SOCIAL WORK WITH ADULTS

SOCIAL WORK WITH ADULTS

JIM ROGERS • LUCY BRIGHT • HELEN DAVIES

MASTERING Social Work Practice

Los Angeles | London | New Delhi
Singapore | Washington DC

Learning Matters
An imprint of SAGE Publications Ltd
1 Oliver's Yard
55 City Road
London EC1Y 1SP

SAGE Publications Inc.
2455 Teller Road
Thousand Oaks, California 91320

SAGE Publications India Pvt Ltd
B 1/I 1 Mohan Cooperative Industrial Area
Mathura Road
New Delhi 110 044

SAGE Publications Asia-Pacific Pte Ltd
3 Church Street
#10-04 Samsung Hub
Singapore 049483

Editor: Kate Wharton
Development editor: Lauren Simpson
Production editor: Chris Marke
Copy editor: Diana Chambers
Proofreader: Sue Edwards
Marketing manager: Tamara Navaratnam
Cover design: Wendy Scott
Typeset by: C&M Digitals (P) Ltd, Chennai, India
Printed and bound in Great Britain by Ashford Colour
Press Ltd.

Library of Congress Control Number: 2015946649

British Library Cataloguing in Publication Data

A catalogue record for this book is available from
the British Library

ISBN 978-1-4739-0755-3 (pbk)
ISBN 978-1-4739-0754-6

At SAGE we take sustainability seriously. Most of our products are printed in the UK using FSC papers and boards.
When we print overseas we ensure sustainable papers are used as measured by the Egmont grading system.
We undertake an annual audit to monitor our sustainability.

Contents

About the authors

Jim Rogers is a senior lecturer in health and social care at the University of Lincoln. He completed professional training as a mental health nurse and worked in that capacity for over twelve years in a range of hospital and community settings. He now co-ordinates the institution's training programmes for approved mental health professionals and best interests assessors. He has conducted research on the Deprivation of Liberty Safeguards with care homes in the region and has a strong interest in issues relating to mental health and mental capacity. Jim co-wrote a text for Learning Matters – *Social Work in a Digital Society* – and has also published academic work relating to complementary therapies, social work and gambling problems, and personal health budgets.

Lucy Bright completed her Masters/Diploma in Social Work in 1993. Since then she has worked in a wide variety of social work settings with adults, as well as spending four years working for a solicitor and specialising in mental health law. Lucy currently works as a best interests assessor and has a particular interest in the Deprivation of Liberty Safeguards and how these have been working in practice since their implementation in 2009.

Helen Davies qualified as a social worker in 1986 and has taught social work students since 1999, while continuing in practice in statutory and voluntary services with adults with learning disabilities. As one of four social work co-ordinators at the Independent Living Fund, she led its work in Wales and Northern Ireland. Helen's current role as senior lecturer at the University of Lincoln includes supporting students to make constructive links between theory and practice.

Acknowledgements

Authorship is often perceived as a solitary endeavour, but it is rarely so. In the case of a co-authored book such as this, debates, discussions and critique of material throughout the gestation period have helped the three of us arrive at something we hope is greater than the sum of three individual parts.

We are grateful to each other for the support during the challenges this process involved. We also wish to express gratitude to colleagues in the worlds of both education and practice who have discussed issues and cases, and stimulated our thinking in relation to the issues in the text. Equally, we are grateful to the many students, on both our undergraduate and post graduate courses, who have engaged with, discussed, and written about these issues.

Helen would like to dedicate this book to Bill and Elsie Davies, appreciatively; Lucy to the service users who have informed and inspired her; and Jim to his family for support and wise guidance.

Chapter 1

Introduction

Whether you are a student in an educational setting or on placement, a newly qualified practitioner, or an experienced practitioner in adult social care, you will no doubt be well aware of the prominence of debates about best interests, about vulnerability and about safeguarding. It is likely that you will have experienced some level of training and debate about these issues and on the subject of mental capacity. You may have also had recent training in relation to the new Care Act 2014 and your workplace may be in the process of beginning to implement that Act and understanding all of the ramifications of it.

The themes noted above are often highlighted as the most important in current adult social care. They were highlighted in the new *Knowledge and Skills Statement* (**KSS**) *for Adult Social Work* which was published in 2015, and local authorities have stated that these are the key areas of skills and knowledge which they consider when recruiting adult social care practitioners.

Tensions and challenges in relation to balancing the need to protect those who are vulnerable in society with the impetus to empower and promote independence have been a constant feature in the history of social work. The current debates and complexities which can arise in relation to safeguarding vulnerable adults and those who lack capacity to make decisions for themselves, while promoting their best interests, can be seen as a new variation on this recurring theme.

Our aim in producing this text was to find a way of elucidating, linking and clarifying these issues in a way that might help those who need to navigate the messy difficulties of practice.

While the text refers where necessary to legislation and policy, there are a number of other existing texts and sources which perform that function well, so the primary emphasis here is on the application of guidance to practice. In order to provide useful and relevant guidance for practice, we use case studies and vignettes where possible to raise questions, and to illustrate issues and dilemmas. While relatively brief written summaries are no real substitute for the realities of practice, they can be useful in clarifying issues, prompting reflection and offering heuristic devices for addressing questions and issues.

Structure of the book

We hold to the notion that, despite some of the difficulties and complexities in application, the best interests principle is a sound one, and one which sits well with the whole set of social work principles and values. We wish to explore the notion of best interests in a broader sense than the merely legal or procedural one which is sometimes the focus. For this reason we begin with a chapter which explores the connection between notions of best interests, promotion of well-being, and the values and ethical basis for such ideas. In this chapter we also explore the often-neglected subject of the well-being and best interests of practitioners. The reason for raising this issue here is straightforward. There is ample evidence that, in an inherently stressful job in which there is a generally a tendency towards very high if not excessive workloads, social care professionals have high levels of stress and burnout. A related and perhaps more significant point is that it is clear that those who have higher levels of stress and lower levels of support are less able to provide empathy or appropriate responses to the vulnerable service users with whom they work, and are less good at appropriate decision making. We therefore explore issues of resilience, mindfulness, stress and coping as aspects of promoting the best interests of self, which in turn leads to more optimal care for service users.

The best interests principle is central to the Mental Capacity Act 2005. In Chapter 3, we explore the history and context of legal regimes for decision making on behalf of those who lack capacity to make decisions for themselves, and show how and why the best interests principle is thought to be the best choice for such a legal framework. The emergence of this legal principle and of the Mental Capacity Act has provided clarity, and these developments are considered by many in the field to be good examples of well-thought out statutes. Nonetheless, it remains the case that practitioners face many challenges of interpretation and potential conflicts of interest between different parties when attempting to implement this law. There are often conflicts between families and professionals, and the challenge of navigating a path which respects the input of family members in relation to best interests decisions when there may be safeguarding allegations furnishes one example of this. Professionals are faced with the responsibility of making decisions about what is ultimately in a person's best interests. Research in social work practice and in other fields (particularly psychology) has assisted in understanding how people make decisions in the real world, and we explore some of these findings, highlighting those which are particularly salient.

This leads on to a consideration in Chapter 4 of the whole of the Mental Capacity Act 2005. To reiterate, our book is not primarily a legal text and there are several others which provide the detail of that law. We refer readers, for example, to Brown, Barber and Martin (2009). We provide some detail on important features of the Act, including the five major principles, but our aim and interest here is to elucidate how different aspects of the Act have been and should be applied in practice. For example, in this chapter we will discuss the dilemma which frequently occurs in relation to judgments and conflicts between the necessity to allow unwise decisions and the duty to protect.

A number of commentators have suggested that the role of advocacy, mandated by certain sections of the Mental Capacity Act, has been relatively neglected in practice. We therefore highlight the importance and benefits of advocacy in this type of work.

Following on from consideration of the Act as a whole, Chapter 5 examines the notion of best interests within the MCA in more detail. Again, while noting the guidance relating to best interests within both the Act and the related *Code of Practice* our focus is on implementation. Thus, we consider issues which are most often highlighted by practitioners, including how to organise and run best interests meetings; who to consult and how to consult them; what to do when agreement is lacking; how and when to use the Court of Protection; and applying best interests decisions with limited resources.

A significant part of the Mental Capacity Act, and one which has proved particularly problematic in terms of legal interpretation, is schedule A1 – the Deprivation of Liberty Safeguards (DOLS). While a full and detailed knowledge of this is perhaps only required by those who go on to train and work in the formal role of 'best interests assessors', it is important that all practitioners understand the nature and purpose of the DOLS regime and how to recognise and work with any deprivation of liberty they come across. There is little guidance elsewhere for practitioners on this subject and in Chapter 6 we provide some advice based on the latest case law, and checklists for practitioners. Given that the DOLS are a result of legal challenges under the Human Rights Act, we also explore the links between social work practice and human rights in a wider sense. We also assess how effective these safeguards are and compare and contrast them with other frameworks and practices which are aimed at safeguarding adults.

Those adults who are deemed to lack the capacity to make decisions for themselves are vulnerable to a variety of potential risks, not only in the extreme and concrete form of being deprived of liberty, but in a range of other ways too. For those who are judged to have decision-making capacity a different set of vulnerabilities can be present. The safeguarding of vulnerable adults has gained increasing prominence in adult social care in recent years. In Chapter 7 we consider how to meld concerns about vulnerability, risk and safeguarding, with considerations of capacity and deprivation of liberty. We examine policy and guidance in this area, and also what case law and serious case reviews can usefully tell us about this subject.

One of the grand narratives which is coming to dominate public services as a whole, but particularly adult social care, is that of personalisation. Chapter 8 explores what this development might mean for the issues that we have discussed so far, and explores how practitioners are facing the challenge of supporting and promoting the choice, control and independence that personalised services can bring while at the same time maintaining their duties to safeguard those who are vulnerable.

Adults who are at risk of harm live in a variety of settings and come into contact with a number of different services. There are some common things but also particular challenges to be addressed in each of these. Chapter 8 particularly highlights some of the issues which occur in relation to the large numbers of adult social care users who live in their own homes or in a family home. In such settings many different professions and support services may have some involvement with the service user, and we consider some of the key issues in relation to partnership and integrated working which can help to maintain both the safety and the independence of service users.

A number of readers will be at the point in their learning journey of making the transition from education to practice. The newly qualified social worker (NQSW) initiative, and the Assessed and Supported Year in Employment (ASYE) have provided useful frameworks of support for those in this position. Chapter 9 provides some material and guidance which is particularly relevant here. We signpost and refer to a range of existing guidance and materials while focusing on a number of themes which may be particularly pertinent. These include developing communication skills for working with adults who lack capacity, and using supervision, critical reflection and feedback well. This last point brings us back full circle to the issues highlighted in Chapter 2 in relation to awareness, critical reflection, supervision and support.

We trust that, whatever your role in adult social care, the text will provide you with useful and relevant information and guidance, and will prompt you to critically assess and reflect both on practice and on the values, ethics, legislation and policy which guide that practice.

Next, we present two case studies which will be referred to regularly throughout the text. There will be questions and practice learning points which illustrate each stage and aspect of the two scenarios. We suggest that you read them carefully at this stage and then refer back to them as required as you progress through the text.

Case Study 1.1

You have received a referral to assess Rosemary Cave, an 82-year-old woman who experiences memory loss. Rosemary is currently an inpatient on an older adults' psychiatric ward, but prior to this had spent six weeks in a general hospital after breaking her femur and a series of urinary tract infections. The multidisciplinary team (MDT) on the ward are asking that Rosemary be assessed with a view to a residential/nursing placement. The referral states that Rosemary is agitated and disorientated on the ward and that she keeps asking when she is going home. Rosemary needs full assistance with her personal care and she now struggles to walk any distance, although she can weight bear.

You make initial contact with the ward to gather further information and establish that Rosemary normally lives with her nephew, Mark Simond, who is her main carer. The nursing staff also tell you that they have made a referral to the safeguarding team, as Mark has been observed trying to get Rosemary to sign some documentation on the ward and they are suspicious of these actions. Nursing staff also inform you that Rosemary needs to be nursed in isolation for large parts of the day, as she has a tendency to lash out at other patients on the ward.

You arrive on the ward to start your assessment. Before you get a chance to speak to Rosemary, a visitor approaches you and tells you that she is Rosemary's daughter (Hilary Gove) and that she has only just found out that her mother is here. Hilary says she and her mother have been estranged for ten years following a family row but that she now wishes to make amends. Hilary states she is very distressed by how her mother is now, asks what the plans are and adds that Mark Simond should not be trusted. You then go to see Rosemary who is sitting alone in a small lounge. The first thing you notice is how similar Rosemary looks to your grandmother to whom you were very close, and who died just a few months ago.

Rosemary seems glad to have company; she talks at length about her childhood home in Exeter and her recollection of the war and air raids. Rosemary is insistent that she needs to find her mother because people are picking on her. Rosemary seems unaware that she is in hospital, but is clear she needs to go home to her mother. You ask Rosemary how she likes it here and she says they are all 'interfering busy-bodies' and should leave her alone. Rosemary makes a grimace when you mention Mark's name, saying he is lazy; she does not respond when you ask her about her daughter. In a moment of clarity Rosemary says she has always hated hospitals and needs to go back to Ash Gardens, her home address. Rosemary then starts crying for her mother again.

You decide you need to speak to the nephew to find out how Rosemary had been managing at home and to offer a carer's assessment. Mark tells you that he had been asking for help for a long time and 'banging his head against a brick wall'. Mark believes he could care for Rosemary at home again if they had extra help including a stair lift, carers in the morning (when Mark does a short shift at the local shop) and three weeks' respite a year. Mark states that he has an Lasting Power of Attorney (LPA) for Rosemary's finances and he does not know what all the fuss with safeguarding is about. Mark tells you that Rosemary is getting worse on the ward and should come home to him as soon as possible. You point out to Mark that the MDT and Hilary are keen for Rosemary to go into a placement as they do not feel she will be safe at home. Mark tells you he has lived with and cared for his aunt for the last eight years and knows her best; he is not very forthcoming when you ask him about how Rosemary came to suffer her broken leg. You feel that Mark is deliberately withholding information.

You have completed various capacity assessments with Rosemary in conjunction with the MDT and the conclusions are that Rosemary lacks capacity to make a decision about remaining on the ward and to decide about where she goes on discharge. It is your assessment that Rosemary has capacity to decide about how she has contact with her nephew and daughter, but the safeguarding team are querying this assessment and feel that contact on the ward should be supervised. Rosemary is always pleased to see you and you find you are spending a lot of time on this case. Your manager suggests you should step back and let the safeguarding team take the lead and await the outcome of the DOLS assessment. There is a backlog of referrals to the team. You feel it is your role to stay involved and advocate for Rosemary.

The best interests meeting for Rosemary is postponed for two weeks while a continuing health-care assessment is undertaken as the MDT state that Rosemary's current levels of agitation mean

(Continued)

(Continued)

that she will need one-to-one support in any placement that is identified for her. Safeguarding have concluded their investigations and have established that Mark does have an LPA for Rosemary's finances, but that they remain suspicious about how Rosemary came to fall and break her leg, although there is no conclusive evidence of physical abuse. A Deprivation of Liberty authorisation is also now in place for eight weeks with recommendations that attempts are made to nurse Rosemary with more one-to-one support in communal areas and that Rosemary is given a period of trial leave at home with a package of support.

After the involvement of an occupational therapist, Rosemary goes home for four days with a package of care and all appears to go well. Rosemary seems calmer at home and is accepting of the help offered. Eventually, Rosemary is discharged home on a more permanent basis. As a social worker, you remain involved at the behest of the safeguarding team, who are monitoring the situation. You still feel uneasy about Mark, who remains evasive and always leaves the house when you visit. Four weeks later you receive a call from the agency providing care, who state that Rosemary had been refusing a wash and when they eventually managed to persuade her, they found bruises on the backs of her thighs.

Comment

This is a difficult and complex case and it is unlikely that as a newly qualified social worker you would be expected to carry this alone, but such situations do occur and demonstrate the increasingly complicated interface of duties and responsibilities in adult social care work. Potential answers and further discussion of all the questions posed are to be found in the remainder of the text.

Case Study 1.2

As a social worker in a community learning disability team, you have been allocated seven cases where reassessment is required following a change in eligibility for service from substantial to critical level.

Carl's case file tells you that he is a 27-year-old man living with his parents and younger sister. He has cerebral palsy but is able to stand and walk. He can manage most personal care tasks and his speech is understood by those who know him well. As a teenager, he was admitted to hospital on several occasions during grand mal fits, but his epilepsy is now well controlled by medication. Carl has a short stay for one weekend out of four in the respite care home attached to the local general hospital. After leaving special school at 19, he attended college full time for two years, but now has a personal assistant three days a week.

You arrange to visit Carl's home at 4pm on Friday evening, when his mother Wendy is home from work. His sister, Louise, is also in with her 4-year-old son, Mark. Wendy is very anxious about the reassessment, and especially the PA hours, which enable her to go out to work. She stresses the high level of supervision she feels Carl needs to ensure that he takes his medication regularly and to keep safe in the house and outside. Louise recounts an incident four months ago when Carl cut his arm when he put his hand through a window and needed emergency treatment at the local hospital. As you try to gain a fuller picture of Carl, they tell you how much he hates to get out of bed or to have a shower, and how he loves to have coins (not notes) in his purse, and enjoys rough-and-tumble play with his nephew.

You discover that Carl has a personal budget, managed by his mother since it was set up five years ago, and that his short stays are health funded. You arrange to meet Carl with his personal assistant at their favourite café, since Wendy has asked them not to use the house during Carl's day-care hours. Martin was a learning support assistant at Carl's school and was asked to 'babysit' for him occasionally in the evening once Carl left school, before becoming his PA three years ago. Carl shakes your hand and shows great interest in your car before starting to eat his bacon and egg, wielding his cutlery very efficiently. When Carl goes to the toilet, Martin shares his frustration that he is not able to do more with Carl because of Wendy's concerns about Carl handling hot liquids and going on public transport. He suggests that her reluctance to enable Carl to become more independent is because Carl's benefits form a large part of the household income since his parents divorced four years ago. As you leave the café, Carl points out Martin's flat in the block opposite and says that he wants a flat there too. Martin confirms that Carl has been saying that he wants to move into his own flat for the last six months and that it has become a standing joke in the family.

Carl's GP is reluctant to give you any medical information without consent. He expresses concern about the strain that caring for Carl puts on Wendy, especially now that her daughter and grandson are living in the household, and suggests that relieving that strain should be your main aim.

You meet Carl's key worker at the short-stay house, once you have gained access through the keypad door system. She tells you how much satisfaction Carl gets from helping to prepare simple meals and from visits to the pub next door, where he is well known and enjoys buying his round. He likes to spend time with staff rather than other people staying in the house and will often take on the staff role, telling people off if he thinks they are misbehaving.

You are also able to spend some time with Carl, supported by his key worker to understand what he is saying. Carl is adamant that he wants to have his own place, like some of his friends from college. He says he wants to see his mother but not for her to be in charge of him any more.

On your return to the office, your manager asks for a progress report on the seven cases allocated to you. You have begun assessments on four so far.

Comment

Some of the issues raised by the two cases, and the legislation and guidance which will inform your decisions, will be familiar to you, including the personalisation agenda, safeguarding and carers' rights. Others may be less familiar.

This book aims to provide the information you need to work your way through the maze of legislation and guidance which needs to be taken into account when seeking to identify an individual's best interests. It also offers you the opportunity to develop robust and reflective decision-making processes in this context and to become aware of yourself as a key element in those processes.

Note on the Professional Capabilities Framework (PCF)

The PCF emerged in 2012 after a lengthy period of work and consultation. Developed by the Social Work Reform Board, the PCF was taken on by the College of Social Work, a body which recently ceased to exist. Some reforms of the PCF were under way in 2015 and it is expected that other expert bodies/organisations will continue some of this work. In the meantime it is expected that the PCF as it stands will remain as a useful framework and steer for educators, students and professionals alike.

Chapter 2

Ethics and vulnerability: service users and social workers

Meeting professional standards

This chapter will help you to develop the following selected capabilities, to the appropriate level, from the social work Professional Capabilities Framework (see Appendix 1).

Professionalism

- Make proactive use of supervision to reflect critically on practice, explore different approaches to your work, support your development across the nine capabilities and understand the boundaries of professional accountability.
- Recognise the impact of self in interaction with others, making appropriate use of personal experience.
- Demonstrate workload management skills and develop the ability to prioritise.
- Recognise and balance your own personal/professional boundaries in response to changing and more complex contexts.
- Develop ways to promote well-being at work, identifying strategies to protect and promote your own well-being and the well-being of others.

Values and ethics

- Understand and apply the profession's ethical principles and legislation, taking account of these in reaching decisions.
- Demonstrate respectful partnership work with service users and carers, eliciting and respecting their needs and views, and promoting their participation in decision making wherever possible.

- Recognise and manage conflicting values and ethical dilemmas to arrive at principled decisions.
- Recognise and promote individuals' rights to autonomy and self-determination.

Knowledge

- Demonstrate a critical understanding of the application to social work of research, theory and knowledge from sociology, social policy, psychology and health.
- Demonstrate a critical understanding of the legal and policy frameworks and guidance that inform and mandate social work practice, recognising the scope for professional judgement.

Critical reflection and analysis

- Show creativity in tackling and solving problems, by considering a range of options to solve dilemmas.

Contexts and organisations

- Work effectively as a member of a team, demonstrating the ability to develop and maintain appropriate professional and inter-professional relationships, managing challenge and conflict with support.
- Taking account of legal, operational and policy contexts, proactively engage with your own organisation and contribute to its evaluation and development.

Introduction

This chapter has two distinct parts. The first deals with various sources of ethical guidance which are available to practitioners to assist them in their work with vulnerable adults. The second part deals with issues of stress and vulnerability in the practitioner and addresses ethical issues which relate to the job role. These include the impact of stress on the ability to act ethically, and also the ethics of imposing unhealthy working practices and conditions on practitioners. What might it mean to work 'ethically' when working with vulnerable adults and what are the relationships between ethics, law, policy and practice in this type of work? We explore these questions and consider how safeguarding and promoting the best interests of practitioners may be integral to safeguarding and promoting the best interests of vulnerable service users.

Every day, social workers along with many other professionals make numerous choices and decisions with and about vulnerable adults. In the cases of those who lack capacity to make particular decisions for themselves there are clear laws, policies and sets of guidelines which are designed to assist those professionals to work effectively and ethically in such situations.

In relation to the 'safeguarding' of vulnerable adults who do have the capacity to make decisions for themselves, there have for some time been clear policy guidance and clear organisational structures in relation to this work. There has been less in the way of legislative levers and mechanisms in relation to adult safeguarding, although this has changed to some degree with the new Care Act 2014.

At intervals throughout the book we present case studies which illustrate typical scenarios encountered in practice. Often these will be used to flag up the ways in which particular points of policy or law have been or should be interpreted in practice. It is often the case, though, that the specific application or interpretation of policy or law in any particular case is not clear or straightforward. In this context it is interesting to note that there has been a move to incorporate values and ethics into the fabric of more recent health and social care legislation, and if not in the actual statute, then into an accompanying code of practice. We see, for example, that the Mental Health Act has a separate code of practice, which has recently been revised (MHA *Code of Practice*, 2015) and that the Mental Capacity Act 2005 and the Care Act 2014 both have values-based principles built into the Acts themselves, as well as having accompanying codes of practice. The authors of the codes attempt to demonstrate, via explication, reference to case law and statute, and also reference to the values and principles of the Acts, and how professionals should proceed to operationalise and utilise the Acts in practice. It is intended that consideration of clear principles and values can provide a steer to help in the interpretation and application of law and policy. In this section we will consider to what extent it is possible and to what extent it is helpful to codify ethics and values, whether within legislation and policy, within government mandated codes of practice, or within frameworks and codes of ethics and practice emanating from professional bodies.

There are a number of valuable texts which address the areas of ethics and values in social work and in the professions more generally. An influential text in health and social care has been the work of Beauchamp and Childress (2008) who advocated what they referred to as 'principlism'. One of the criticisms sometimes levelled at debates about the application of ethical principles to the work of the care professions is that they are too abstract. Beauchamp and Childress attempted to move beyond a number of texts which presented classical ethical theories as guides for practice, and to furnish something more pragmatic which would assist professionals in approaching the complex and changing realities of decision making in practice. Their approach incorporates principles which have been central to modern liberal democratic societies, such as the autonomy of the individual person and the right of each individual to receive justice. Other elements spring from the moral position advocated by the tradition of virtue ethics, including the ideas that we should always strive for non-maleficence (not doing harm) and beneficence (doing good).

There are many issues relating to adult safeguarding, judgements about mental capacity and deprivation of liberty, for which policy and law do not afford crystal-clear guidance. It may be that there are differing or even conflicting case law judgments or that policy does not have anything to say about the very specific issue that you are grappling with. Can 'principlism' or any other ethical approach help practitioners in these situations?

One respected commentator on social work has noted, in relation to judgments about protection and capacity: *I think that social workers sometimes get confused about this and imagine that, if only they gathered enough information these difficult decisions would somehow solve themselves as if they were purely technical problems* (Beckett, 2006, p27). He goes on to discuss the importance of ethics and values for informing such decisions.

Of course, ethics and values must be coupled with knowledge and skills. The most ethical and good person would be a poor and potentially dangerous practitioner if they had no knowledge of the job role, or of the options available to them – the powers and duties which their role afforded, or the services and options available to them in practice. Good intentions are an insufficient basis on which to make complex assessment and care decisions. On the other hand, we would not trust the person with the most detailed knowledge and apparent technical competence if they appeared to have no morals or ethics at all.

The following case study and related commentary illustrate how ethical frameworks may help to provide a compass to guide decision making in a typical practice situation.

Case Study 2.1

Mr B is 77 years old and has been resident in a care home in the South of England for several years. He has steadily progressive dementia. The fees for the care home have been paid by the local authority. After recent cuts to the social care budget, coupled with an increase in the fee rate set by the home, the local authority has said that it intends to move Mr B, along with several other residents, to a home which has significantly lower fees. That home is one hundred miles away. You have been asked to conduct a review of the care of Mr B, with a view to facilitating the move to the new care home. You find that Mr B has one family member, an only daughter who lives a short bus ride away from the current care home and visits once a week. The daughter, Mrs S, has two part-time jobs. She is not in a position financially to 'top up' the fees for the current home, and would find it very difficult to find the time or money to visit her father should he be moved to the proposed new care home.

Comment

Applying the Beauchamp and Childress ethical framework might lead to the following considerations.

Respect for autonomy

This means taking into account the person's views about the situation. Of course, there are many reasons why a person may not be able to make a fully autonomous decision. A person with dementia may well lack the capacity to make an informed decision about a change of accommodation. However, reflecting the importance of this ethical principle, the Mental Capacity Act states very clearly that individuals should make their own autonomous decisions as far as possible. Where they are judged to lack the mental capacity to make a particular decision, they should still be involved as far as possible in the consultation about the decision. Thus, the principle of autonomy is enshrined in the first principles of the Mental Capacity Act. Mr B has become distressed when any suggestions about him moving have been raised and it is clear that, were he able to do so, he would not make an autonomous decision to move.

Beneficence

The professional should always consider what might be of most benefit to the person. Often it is necessary to consider both the short-term and the long-term aspects of this. A move from independent living to a care home is often distressing and traumatic in the short term, but the long-term benefits may considerably outweigh these factors in terms of the safety and well-being of the individual. In relation to the situation of Mr B, who has been settled at home A for some years, you may be aware of concerns which are frequently expressed in the media and by campaign groups about the impact of care home closures and moves.

Research indicates that the impact of care home moves varies greatly and may be much to do with how the process is planned for and managed (Williams and Netten, 2003). A recent review of the evidence in relation to forced relocation between homes found that outcomes were negative in terms of stress, health and survival rates when moves were poorly planned and casually implemented. In contrast, positive outcomes from well-planned and co-ordinated moves included *no change in mortality rate, physical or mental health, or quality of life, reduced falls and use of restraint, and increased social contact, community access and psycho-social wellbeing* (Holder and Jolley, 2012, p301).

This illustrates the importance of knowledge and use of research findings in informing an ethically based practice.

Non-maleficence

This refers to the principle of not doing any harm to the person. Again, reference to knowledge and research findings about potential harms of moves between care homes is relevant here. In relation to both beneficence and non-maleficence you may also question what level of benefit and what level of emotional harm to Mr B may be caused if his only family member was able to visit far less often. Careful consideration of the nature of the relationship would be necessary here.

Justice

This is usually taken to refer to the fair sharing of resources and benefits among members of society. At one level this might mean considering that the proposed move is just, since the fee savings in relation to this small number of individuals will allow care to be purchased for more members of society. Banks discusses the different responsibilities that the social work role encompasses, including those towards employers, and explores how a moral/ethical duty to ensure fair and equitable distribution of resources or to provide social control may conflict with a duty to the individual. Banks talks about such conflicts as ethical problems and dilemmas and sees them as inherent to the practice of social work:

> *The reasons for this arise from its role as a public service profession dealing with vulnerable and marginalised service users who need to be able to trust the worker and be protected from exploitation; and also from its position in many countries as part of state welfare provision, which is itself based on contradictory aims and values – care and control, capital accumulation and legitimation, protection of individual rights and promotion of public welfare.*

(Banks, 2012, p34)

One of the major differences between the health professions and social work is sometimes seen as the latter's commitment to social justice. It cannot be assumed, of course, that there is agreement about the nature and importance of social justice. It is a concept which arose from socialist movements, and as the United Nations' explanation of the concept makes clear, it is an inherently political notion. They note that *By the mid-twentieth century, the concept of social justice had become central to the ideologies and programmes of virtually all the leftist and centrist political parties around the world* (United Nations, 2006, 12). Those whose politics lie more to the right see a different role for the state, and have different conceptions about how and to what extent welfare regimes should operate. They do not subscribe to the notion of social justice, which usually includes explicit reference to the redistribution of resources and wealth within a society. As can be seen in the case above, issues of the distribution and redistribution of resources are pertinent to many individual decisions that practitioners make.

There have been a number of attempts over the years to explicitly codify commitments to social justice, as can be seen in various iterations of professional codes of ethics in social work in the UK. The most recent examples include statements by bodies which represent the profession in various ways.

The College of Social Work, the body set up in 2013 to promote and enhance the profession, asks its members to subscribe to a commitment to *promote social justice and display compassion and respect in my professional practice.* The point is elaborated in the statement which follows:

> I acknowledge that social work is founded on principles of social justice and I will therefore seek to understand, and promote through my work, outcomes that support human dignity and the respect of each member of society for their fellow human beings. I will challenge, in an appropriate manner, discrimination and stigmatisation wherever I encounter it.

> (The College of Social Work, 2013b, p2)

The British Association of Social Workers (BASW) is equally explicit in the statements about social justice. In the background to its 2012 *Code of Ethics* it suggests the following:

> Human rights and social justice serve as the motivation and justification for social work action. In solidarity with those who are disadvantaged, the profession strives to alleviate poverty and to work with vulnerable and oppressed people in order to promote social inclusion.

> (BASW, 2012, p5)

It notes that its code is binding on all BASW members.

There are interesting and contrasting views about whether and to what extent professionals have a moral and ethical duty to lobby and advocate on matters of policy as well as in relation to individual service users. Hugman (2005) suggests that the professions have a *social mandate* to practise with individuals and families as they do, a mandate which is given from law, bureaucratic decision, or the choices of consumers. Some authors believe that the professions 'overstep' this social mandate when collectively expressing criticism of institutional or government policy (Clarke, 1998, p248). Others, with more critical or radical leanings, believe that it is expressly part of the function of a profession such as social work to challenge policy which is seen as reinforcing discrimination or poverty, or is maintaining unequal power structures. Indeed, those who adopt such views advocate that this is the only 'ethical' approach to practise.

The codes referred to above are a significant feature of the caring professions and are given high regard and attention in professional training programmes. As suggested above in relation to social justice, it is likely that what can and should be expressed in professional codes will always be subject to vigorous debate and disagreement. However, you are expected to be cognisant of and compliant with the code of your profession at the time in which you are practising. You will note from the items from the Professional Capabilities Framework which head this chapter that the framework is closely linked to codes of ethics. Placing these statements in student textbooks, and using and debating them in various educational activities, are elements in the professional socialisation which aims to ensure that social work graduates are familiar with and committed to these values and approaches.

Returning to the case study on page 12, we have considered the application of one framework to the work with Mr B. What might other 'ethical' perspectives add? The Mental Capacity Act is considered in detail in Chapter 5. Note that the Act has a set of ethically based principles enshrined within it. It is clear that these principles, including the directives to assume capacity unless proven otherwise and to involve the person as much as possible in any decisions made about them, give force to the 'respect for autonomy' principle which, as Beauchamp and Childress noted in their framework, is culturally very highly valued in modern liberal democratic societies.

You may also think that human rights legislation is important here. In particular, Article 8 of the European Convention, the right to private and family life, has a significant bearing in this case. The Convention provides another example of codifying and providing a framework of ethics. Since public bodies must uphold the Convention rights of citizens, the Human Rights Act provides one possible avenue for challenging decisions made in cases such as those of Mr B.

We have here considered a broad ethical framework and have touched on debates about the helpfulness of professional codes of ethics to practitioners. There are, of course, many other ethical frameworks which might be applied, and readers are encouraged to explore the extensive literature on ethics in the caring professions for further guidance.

In the remainder of this chapter we put centre-stage issues of potential vulnerability for the practitioner and issues relating to the best interests and well-being of the practitioner. These are issues which do not usually feature in considerations of ethics in relation to practice, but we believe that this focus is fully justified for the following reasons.

First, as noted above, social work training and the professional codes which graduates sign up to place a significant emphasis on values and ethics. On entering practice it often becomes clear that it is difficult to uphold these values. While some find ways to accommodate to these realities and thrive as practitioners (Wendt et al., 2011), the cognitive dissonance, frustration, guilt and other responses to this dilemma are factors which can lead to significant stress and burnout in others (Rushton, 1987; Lloyd et al., 2002).

Second, although issues of stress and burnout have been highlighted in many studies of social work (Coyle et al., 2005), they tend to be overlooked or not given a great deal of attention in the educational literature for the profession. That literature tends to prioritise legal and policy frameworks and practice skills, and both the emotional labour which is an inherent part of the role (Gorman, 2000; Leeson, 2010) and the emotional impact of that role (Dwyer, 2007) are given scant attention in many texts. A number of practitioner accounts also suggest that insufficient attention is paid to these issues during training. Third, there are strong and possibly two-way relationships between stress and decision making, and between stress, empathy, compassion and ethical practice.

Research Summary 2.1

Stress, burnout and the helping professions

What do we know about stress and the care professions? The reality of practice is that factors which may contribute to stress and burnout are ever present in most workplace contexts, and the presence of factors which can lessen the likelihood of stress and burnout varies widely. UK and international studies report consistently high levels of stress in social work (Coyle et al., 2005) and that social workers experience higher levels of work-related stress and burnout than many other occupational groups (Grant and Kinman, 2013)

The strains of the emotional labour of the job contribute to stress and burnout in social work (Gregor, 2010). The high workloads which tend to constitute social work practice and variable quality of supervision and management are other significant factors which have been flagged up in research studies (Tham and Meagher, 2009). Reviews have summarised clearly both the personal and the occupational factors which lead to stress and burnout in social work (Siebert, 2005) and in nursing (Gelsema et al., 2006). These studies have elucidated not only the factors involved but the very high levels of the problem within those professions. Siebert's study, for example, found that 75 per cent of social workers reported burnout at some stage of their career (Siebert, 2005). In the same period a study by Evans et al. (2005) indicated that in the UK the specific group of social workers practising in mental health services reported surprisingly high levels of mental distress, with 60 per cent of respondents classified as probable cases of common mental disorders according to scores on the well-validated General Health Questionnaire (GHQ-12). High levels of stress and burnout may, of course, lead to people leaving the job. Researchers at the Personal Social Services Research Unit (PSSRU) attempted to quantify this and came to the stark conclusion that the average working life of a qualified social worker is just eight years, and that this compares to 15 years for nurses, 25 for doctors and 28 for pharmacists (Curtis et al., 2009). The researchers found that workplace stress was the most commonly cited reason for leaving the profession.

It might be thought that these discussions are relevant to a text about stress management but are tangential to discussions of working with vulnerable adults. In fact, these issues are important to those discussions for the reason that stress has significant effects not only on the well-being of a practitioner but also on how they practise. The over-stressed practitioner is more likely to be less empathic and to make less good decisions. Recent research confirms that raised stress hormones are highly correlated with reduced empathy, and many studies have shown that raised levels of the same stress hormones impair decision making (Starcke and Brand, 2012).

The research on stress and decision making is fairly consistent, but there are some complexities and differences which should be noted. For example, males seem to be more likely to make risky decisions when under stress and females to be more risk averse (Mather and Lighthall, 2012).

Looking at the issue from another perspective, there is also some fairly clear evidence that the need to repeatedly make difficult ethical decisions may be a risk factor for stress and burnout in professionals (Texeira et al., 2014).

Comment

A number of research studies conducted across a number of different helping professions point to the conclusions that being overly stressed from whatever cause can lead to less effective and less ethical decision making, but also that the role requirement to repeatedly make ethical decisions may be a risk factor for stress and burnout.

It is crucial both to recognise these facts and to explore potential mechanisms for tackling these problems. One route to helping individuals to recognise stress and address their own needs is through a focus on teaching self-care in academic settings (e.g. Christopher et al., 2006) and through professional development programmes (Shapiro et al., 2007). In social work, the inclusion of training in techniques such as mindfulness in undergraduate programmes (see below) and in the workplace demonstrates clear benefits for practitioners in relation to their own well-being and their effectiveness in the job.

Empathy and vulnerability

Your training to date will have provided you with some level of knowledge and skills in relation to listening and counselling. The concept of empathy is fundamental to helping relationships and is given primacy in all the varied counselling and psychotherapy theories and schools of training. It is often assumed, implicitly or explicitly, that the more empathic a person can be, the better the outcomes and levels of satisfaction will be in terms of helping relationships.

However, it is important to note that empathy is, in fact, a multidimensional entity, with different emotional and cognitive facets. Davis (1980) identified at least three key components: perspective taking – the ability to imagine and adopt the perspective of other people; empathic concern – the ability to experience feelings of warmth, compassion and concern for others; and empathic distress – the experience of feeling anxiety and discomfort when hearing about the difficult experiences of others.

Where the experience of empathic distress is high, the well-being of the helper can suffer. A number of authors have highlighted the risks of being emotionally over-involved with others in terms of compassion fatigue and burnout, and empathic distress may be a significant element in this.

Recent research by Grant and Kinman (2013, 2014) provided some very useful insights into the ways in which the different facets of empathy demonstrated by social workers impacted on their own well-being. They noted that the demonstration of both empathic concern and perspective taking appears to enhance resilience and well-being, while the experience of empathic distress has the opposite effect, with negative consequences for the psychological well-being of the practitioner (Grant and Kinman, 2014, p28).

Case Study 2.2

Jan had worked in a local authority day centre for 18 years. She was very committed to her job and to the service users, and was well liked, being seen as a very warm and caring person. Over the years she had experienced several periods of feeling down and overwhelmed by the job. During the most recent episode she was off work for three months and had been diagnosed with depression.

She said that she resented managers in the authority for being able to make decisions with a pen and remove vital services or increase charges for service users. She said: *It is not the managers that lie awake at night worrying about how our frail eighty year olds are going to survive when they can no longer afford any help ... it's me that's having the nightmares, picturing them alone and vulnerable and with no one arriving at their door with help.*

Comment

The ability to respond with empathic concern and to be able to take the other person's perspective, without over-identifying with them, seems to be a crucial skill in maintaining resilience and being effective in the job. The nature of working in social care means that we will regularly come face to face with people suffering real hardship and distress. In order to be a positive presence in their lives it is vital that we can demonstrate empathic concern and provide support that makes a difference to their lives, without being overwhelmed by the process.

Mindfulness, stress and resilience

There is a range of techniques and practices which can be learned and which have a strong evidence base for being useful in terms of reducing stress and increasing resilience. Of those, one that has been gaining particular attention is that of Mindfulness-Based Stress Reduction (MBSR). Since Jon Kabat-Zinn first developed this approach at the University of Massachusetts medical centre in 1979, it has been developed, researched and introduced to people on an ever-increasing scale. He defined mindfulness as *paying attention in a particular way; on purpose, in the present moment, and non judgmentally* (Kabat-Zinn, 1994).

Contemplation is a feature of many religious and philosophic traditions. The tradition from which modern 'mindfulness' techniques emerged is the Buddhist one and, as their scholars have suggested for millennia, the mind can be trained via the practice of regular meditation. The results of learning to pay attention to whatever presents by using moment-to-moment awareness, with an attitude of non-judgement, seem to be many and varied. Indeed, the most impressive thing about mindfulness is the cascade of research studies that continue to be produced worldwide, which both attest to the benefits of the approach and elucidate more of the mechanisms and facets of mindfulness which make it effective.

Given that stress can lead to less effective and less ethical decision making, can mindfulness, as well as reducing stress, also help decision-making ability? Research studies are indeed beginning to show that regular practice of mindfulness meditation can do just that. Shapiro et al. (2012) confirmed the findings of a raft of studies that participation in an MBSR programme leads to measurable improvements in well-being after two months. What they further demonstrated was that MBSR may also *facilitate moral reasoning and decision making in adults* (Shapiro et al., 2012).

Mindfulness in social work education and practice

A number of researchers have attempted to introduce mindfulness into social work training programmes and practice. In one example, McGarrigle and Walsh found that a typical mindfulness training programme improved self-care and reduced stress in practising social workers (McGarrigle and Walsh, 2011).

A good deal of social work literature alludes to the importance of reflective practice. You will not doubt be familiar with the requirement to reflect from your experiences in your career so far, whether on placement as a student, or in a social work role. One thing that is sometimes missing from these exhortations to be reflective is a sense of how to best go about it and what exactly to reflect on.

Mishna and Bogo (2007) recently described the potential benefits of the act of mindfulness in relation to reflective practice in social work. Mindfulness training instils habits of reflecting in a particular non-judgemental way on experience, and a number of studies have assessed the extent to which mindfulness links with the ability to be reflective, and the consequences of any such link. Discussing the need for the social work educator to be reflective and 'mindful', particularly when dealing with subjects such as diversity which are likely to raise a range of responses and strong emotions in a classroom, the authors note a number of examples in which habits of mindfulness assisted educators in reflecting in the moment and managing the classroom situation effectively.

A central and explicit tenet of social work ethics and values has been that of 'anti-oppressive practice'. A commitment to social justice demands the reduction of prejudice towards and the oppression of those who are disadvantaged in society. In some texts the exhortations to be anti-oppressive are more evident than any realistic guidance on how to deal with bias and prejudice towards others and to reduce the 'oppression' which exists.

A recent study with a group of 72 students found that mindfulness can mitigate bias and prejudice. The students, who were not told beforehand the purpose of the research, were given the Implicit Assumptions Test – this measures how quickly people associate value judgement words such as good or bad with people from different social groups, including those with disabilities and those from different ethnic and racial groups. Such associations and value judgements are often made unconsciously. However, and as this study indicated, this does not mean that they are not malleable and open to change. Here researchers found that after listening to guidance on a short mindfulness meditation, students were less likely to exhibit bias, as measured by the IAT, to black people and to older people, than those who listened to a recording about natural history for a similar period of time (Lueke and Gibson, 2014).

A possibly significant caveat should be added to this discussion about self-care and the potential for increasing ethical decision-making capacity and empathy via self-care and the development of traits such as mindfulness and emotional intelligence. Maslach (2003) suggested that occupational factors are more significant than individual ones in relation to stress in care professionals. This might mean that individual stress-management techniques and individual traits are no substitute for making workplaces more healthy and conducive to the kinds of ethical care practices that we might wish for. More critical voices have used this evidence to suggest that the trend for the uptake in mindfulness training, particularly by organisations, simply reflects cynical attempts to deflect attention away from excessive workloads, excessive working hours and poor workplace cultures. This argument suggests that it is wrong to simply teach a few 'tricks' which might help people to put up with more stress and strain than should be allowed in the workplace. Rather, attention should be focused on making workplaces more healthy places, and on ensuring healthy workloads and adequate resources.

It is certainly the case that structural factors can play a significant role in increasing the level of what has been termed 'moral stress' and that this in turn can lead to burnout. The literature on moral stress refers to 'no-win' situations; these often refer to practice dilemmas in which any of the possible or available options are less than ideal and may not resolve problems. Structural factors, including a lack of resources, excessive caseloads and institutionalised prejudices may place a 'moral burden' on the practitioner who wishes to do the right thing but does not have the authority or resources to make it happen. In such a situation, Tessman (2005) suggests that practitioners will experience either indifference or anguish and that this will eventually lead to what others have described as 'compassion fatigue' (Forster, 2009).

Recall the case study on page 12 in relation to Mr B. This scenario has become increasingly common and many social workers are faced with having to choose from a limited number of less than ideal choices in terms of arranging care for individuals, due to steadily reducing resources.

A constructive approach would acknowledge that all this is best viewed not as an either/or situation but as a both/and situation. Individuals can take steps to improve their own mindfulness and well-being while at the same time advocating for better work practices and environments, more manageable caseloads and better outcomes for service users.

Indeed, mindfulness is largely about greater awareness and a 'mindful' practitioner may be more aware and critical of those things which are dysfunctional in a workplace. We concur with others writing on the subject who say *nor do we wish the promotion of subjective well-being and the use of mindfulness practices to be tools to placate workers into subservient acceptance of those things that are deeply problematic about practice or the social problems associated with it. Rather, mindfulness, and subjective well-being, can be key resources that help social workers practise more effectively, and critically* (Shier and Graham, 2011).

Becoming a social worker

The research relating to stress and the social work profession has noted that in some ways the training period can be more stressful than qualified practice (Grant and Kinman, 2013).

The conflicting demands of being a student and developing as an autonomous professional can be particularly difficult (Pearcey and Elliott, 2004). One student at this stage of the learning journey in social work described it as follows:

> *I've done a degree before here in psychology which is a tough degree too [.] I've also worked in stressful jobs … in residential childcare … in hospital … which I know I can handle but … I never had any anxiety levels like this.*

> (Wilson and Kelly, 2012, p6)

These challenges can be significant. However, if you are in the final stages of a degree programme or you are a qualified social worker, you have already demonstrated significant coping abilities and the capacity to manage high workloads as evidenced by the fact that you have completed a demanding academic programme and have managed caseloads, whether on a placement or in practice.

The structures and processes for supporting social workers at the stage of transition from student to practitioner are considered in more detail in Chapter 9, which focuses on the Assessed and Supported Year in Employment (ASYE).

Given the challenges at all stages of the social work career, managing workloads, maintaining self-care practices and learning techniques such as mindfulness may be very helpful. These things can help to ensure that you maintain your own well-being and practice ethically so that you can best ensure the welfare of those vulnerable people with whom you work.

Chapter Summary

Social work training has a significant emphasis on values and ethics. In this chapter we considered some of the sources of ethical guidance for working with vulnerable adults, including ethical frameworks, professional codes of practice and legislation and associated codes of practice.

Values and ethics are demonstrated in the way that a person behaves and acts and the decisions that they make. A person who is stressed is more likely to make unethical and less effective decisions. In the second part of this chapter we detailed some of the findings about stress in social work practice and examined some of the ways in which stress can be managed and reduced. The next chapter will examine influences on decision making in more detail.

Further Reading

Banks, S (2012) *Ethics and Values in Social Work.* London: Palgrave Macmillan.

Sarah Banks's book remains one of the best sources for social workers wishing to develop a greater understanding of ethics in relation to their profession. It is clear but with nuanced and sophisticated applications of a range of ethical theories to social work practice issues.

Grant, L and Kinman, G (2014) *Developing Resilience for Social Work Practice.* London: Palgrave Macmillan.

This is an excellent contemporary summary of much of the research on social work practice and a practical guide to a range of self-care techniques and strategies.

Chapter 3

Decision making in work with vulnerable adults

Meeting professional standards

This chapter will help you to develop the following selected capabilities, to the appropriate level, from the social work Professional Capabilities Framework.

Professionalism

- Recognise the impact of self in interaction with others, making appropriate use of personal experience.

Values and ethics

- Understand and apply the profession's ethical principles and legislation, taking account of these in reaching decisions.

Rights, justice and economic well-being

- Understand how legislation and guidance can advance or constrain people's rights and recognise how the law may be used to protect or advance their rights and entitlements.

Knowledge

- Demonstrate a critical understanding of the application to social work of research, theory and knowledge from sociology, social policy, psychology and health.
- Demonstrate a critical understanding of the legal and policy frameworks and guidance that inform and mandate social work practice, recognising the scope for professional judgement.

Critical reflection and analysis

- Inform decision making through the identification and gathering of information from multiple sources, actively seeking new sources.

- Demonstrate a holistic approach to the identification of needs, circumstances, rights, strengths and risks.

Introduction

In this chapter we begin to look at the role of some key legal frameworks in assisting decision makers, some key case law which has implications for practice, and also some of the lessons which can be learned from research from a number of disciplines about human decision making. We begin by taking a step back to assess the ways in which decisions have been taken in the past in relation to those who we would now view as vulnerable adults, and in particular those judged as lacking capacity to make decisions for themselves – a group who will be the particular focus of this chapter. The Mental Capacity Act (MCA) 2005 has introduced significant and welcome safeguards for many vulnerable adults and, while there remain too many instances of professionals making decisions on behalf of others without properly consulting or assessing capacity, we have certainly moved on from the times when the apparently omnipotent and omniscient professional would regularly make life-changing decisions for people without consulting or informing them or their families in advance. History can be a great teacher, and a brief perusal of some of the debates and practices in relation to decisions made on behalf of the incapacitated in previous eras may aid in understanding how we arrived at the current position, and may also help to clarify the particular strengths of the MCA.

The Care Act 2014 has also introduced a range of new standards and powers which are important for working with vulnerable adults and which have strengthened the approach to 'safeguarding' such adults in practice. We will assess some of the implications of the Act and the guidance it provides for making decisions when working with the vulnerable, whether they have capacity or not. Please also refer to Chapter 7 for more detailed guidance on working with vulnerable adults.

Decision making in situations of complexity and uncertainty can be driven by fear and anxiety about the consequences of acting or not acting in particular circumstances. Professionals may be concerned about having to appear in court to justify their actions; being subject to complaints from service users, carers or family members; or being subject to criticisms from managers and supervisors. The legal frameworks of the MCA and the Care Act give clear guidance but also clear legal protection and professional justification for workers in relation to their decision making. While this legal protection should not be used as a screen to deflect attention from poor decision making and abuse of power, it should give the practitioner who follows the principles of the Acts carefully some confidence in their work and their judgements.

At the same time as legal and policy frameworks have evolved, our understanding of the realities of human decision making has also evolved significantly. Psychological research in recent decades has provided significant and sometimes surprising insights into how adults make decisions in the real world. Particularly in situations of uncertainty and hurry, people are vulnerable to a number of typical errors of judgement. An informed awareness of such vulnerabilities and habits may help in avoiding some of them. Research with social workers and other professionals in such situations has enabled a more sophisticated understanding of these processes to emerge. We will examine some of the useful messages and insights from such research and try to apply them to issues of safeguarding and mental capacity.

Decision making and social work

As O'Sullivan (2010) suggests, *decision making is a core professional activity at the heart of social work, with much of what social workers do involving making decisions with others* (p1). There is a significant body of literature which focuses on the nature and practice of decision making in social work (Banks, 2006; Parton 2001). Much of this rightly puts significant emphasis on giving primacy to the views and wishes of service users, and using a framework of values and skills to work with and empower individuals and families. There is perhaps less guidance in that literature on approaches to decision making in situations in which a person lacks the capacity to make the decision and may have varying or limited capacity to engage in any meaningful discussion about the relevant decision. We will consider in this chapter some of the approaches which have emerged in relation to this issue, both from guidance issued by professional bodies and from a substantial body of case law, as well as recent statutory frameworks such as the MCA and the Care Act. Those statutes have a clear focus on empowerment and endeavour to enshrine the rights-based principles which human rights legislation and conventions have brought to bear within UK legislation. Our legislation and policy has been moving from a position of encouraging the participation of service users and carers in decision making (which can be seen in the reforms brought in by the NHS and Community Care Act 1990 and the *Code of Practice* to the Mental Health Act 1983, for example) to one of giving some real choice and control to people in relation to decisions over their care and treatment. We may agree that *social workers should involve service users to the fullest level in decision making* (O'Sullivan, 2010, p56). However, it should be recognised that the question of how to uphold rights and to maximise choice and control for people who lack capacity to varying degrees remains an interesting and difficult challenge for practitioners.

Questions of mental capacity arise in a range of settings. Typically, social workers will be assessing the mental capacity of individuals with learning disabilities, those with dementia, and those with a variety of brain injuries caused by trauma or illness. The cultures and practices which have developed in relation to working with each of the service user groups can be quite distinctive, and the ways in which individuals and multidisciplinary teams set about working with and making decisions for people in the different service settings may be quite different.

The tension between the imperatives to protect and safeguard the vulnerable on one hand and to empower and promote independence on the other is perhaps one of the most discussed in social work (Wendt and Seymour, 2010). This tension is seen clearly when comparing the intentions of recent legislation with the realities of practice in different settings.

For example, the House of Lords Select Committee produced in 2014 a 'post-legislative scrutiny report' based on an in-depth investigation of the operation of the MCA. After questioning 61 witnesses and scrutinising over 200 written submissions it noted that:

> *A consistent theme in the evidence was the tension between the empowerment which the Act was designed to deliver, and the tendency of professionals to use the Act for safeguarding purposes. Prevailing professional cultures of risk aversion and paternalism have inhibited the aspiration of empowerment from being realised.*
>
> (House of Lords, 2014, para. 15)

Key statutes and policy documents do provide guidance which should be applied consistently across all practice settings. It was hoped that the MCA would provide a clear framework for doing so, and another such national framework was introduced by the Care Act 2014.

A third significant policy driver is, of course, personalisation and it should be noted that a lack of capacity is not necessarily a barrier to a person having some choice over their care and having a personal budget which can be managed on their behalf – usually by a family member. The personalisation drive is also seen in the language and policy direction which the Care Act brings in.

A key lesson from the review of the MCA mentioned above is perhaps the difficulty of ensuring that a national legislative framework is put into practice in the intended way in a range of quite different practice settings. The ways in which individual practitioners make decisions can be influenced more by training, workplace cultures, deference to those perceived to have more power, professional ethics and a range of factors other than the legislative framework.

The MCA has been in operation for some seven years with mixed results in terms of its impact on practice. For the MCA to be more widely and uniformly implemented, it perhaps needs to be more embedded into different workplace cultures. Training is one method of beginning to achieve this, though training needs to focus on relevant case studies and methods of handling the ambiguities and complexities which arise, as well as on the basic principles of the Act. The Care Act is new and there has been less opportunity to assess its impact and any unforeseen consequences of the changes it introduces.

Research Summary 3.1

Reports and research findings which point to a lack of consistency in professional decision making are not new. Britner and Mossler (2002) discuss this in relation to child protection social work, and recent work commissioned by the UK government found that decision making in social work suffers from a number of endemic problems, including a lack of evidence or a failure to provide it to social workers in order to assist them in making consistent decisions (Kirkman and Melrose, 2014). In view of this, many authors recommend more structured approaches, with the use of decision tools to help to shape more consistent professional practice (Gawande, 2010). There is more information about relevant decision tools in Chapters 4 (MCA), 6 (Deprivation of Liberty Safeguards) and 7 (vulnerable adults), together with some examples.

There is no doubt that structures and decision tools can provide useful aids to decision making but, as many authors note, they cannot in themselves provide definitive answers to complex human problems. Dreyfus and Dreyfus (1986) warn against the 'Hamlet' model of decision making, by which they mean a detached, deliberate and sometimes agonised consideration of each option in isolation in a linear and rational way. To do or not to do? Some researchers have concluded that the uncritical use of decision tools can impair professional development, if not used wisely (Gillingham, 2011), and this point has been echoed in serious case reviews. Lord Laming made the same point in his review of the Baby P case (Laming, 2009).

Comment

While it is clear that greater consistency is desirable in relation to implementing the principles of statutes such as the MCA and the Care Act, we need to be mindful that decision making in relation to issues of care and treatment is always going to be complex and consistency in relation to principles will not lead to identical decisions in each practice situation.

Allen (1993, p46) suggests that moral decisions are made through active dialogue and this reminds us that when trying to make decisions in relation to issues which involve ethical dilemmas and differing opinions we cannot sit down in isolation with a checklist and make that decision alone. We have to engage in a process of discussion and ongoing debate. We also have to be able to tolerate ambiguity and uncertainty. We should try to include those who lack capacity as far as possible in the process, and we should continue to involve carers and advocates in the process. In Chapter 5 we will say more about the collective aspects of 'best interests' decision making and the importance of consulting and debating with a range of people before arriving at a decision.

The discussions in the previous chapter are also relevant here. Moral decisions cannot be informed only by rational calculation but must also be driven by ethical imperatives such as compassion, justice and a commitment to do no harm. The debate instigated by feminist scholars is also relevant here, in emphasising that ethical decision making needs to be situated in the context of a specific relationship of care between a care giver and care recipient. Authors such as Gilligan (1982) suggest that ethics and morality have to be understood in terms of relationships rather than as issues of personal autonomy. From this perspective, abstract principles can never provide a satisfactory basis on which to make ethical decisions. Such decisions can only be made in a health and social care setting when the decision maker has a relationship with and knowledge of the individual with whom they wish to arrive at a decision.

Activity 3.1

Consider again the situation of Rosemary (see pages 4–6). If you were tasked with assessing Rosemary while she was on the hospital ward with a view to making decisions about her capacity, her care and her residence how would you set about the process?

Comment

We hope that you would default to a consideration of a need for an assessment of capacity. This should always be a starting point in relation to any case in which there are any clues that capacity might be lacking. Using the two-stage test of capacity as set out in the MCA for each care and residence decision would be appropriate practice. Following the assessment of capacity, and if Rosemary were deemed to lack capacity, the checklist from section 4 of the MCA should be used to help determine her 'best interests'. The point to emphasise here is that, while the checklists in the MCA and related Code of Practice are very helpful, you may be still be left with significant uncertainty as to how to act. Thinking clearly about the most 'ethical' option can provide an additional steer to assist in such decision making, and it will be through a process of dialogue with Rosemary and those involved in her care that a sense of the ethical thing to do will emerge.

Before assessing in more detail some key research findings about human decision making, we will outline the development of the philosophy and approaches which underpin the legal and policy framework that now exist in the UK in relation to decision making where a person may be vulnerable through a lack of capacity to make their own decisions.

The development of a legal framework: *parens patriae*, common law and the doctrine of necessity

Since the MCA is seen as central to issues of decision making with those who may lack capacity, what are the principles which underpin the Act and how did they develop?

English law states that consent must be obtained before any treatment or procedure can lawfully be carried out. Otherwise, it may be that any direct contact with the individual risks being an offence under the assault and battery laws.

One of the oldest protections under English law is given to liberty. Some 800 years ago Magna Carta stated that *No free man shall be seized or imprisoned or stripped of his rights or possessions, or outlawed or exiled … except by the lawful judgement of his equals or by the law of the land* (British Library, 2014, clause 39). While most of the 63 clauses in that document have not remained relevant or valid, this is one of three which has. In the ensuing period, 'common law' has provided the legal protection for liberty as envisaged by Magna Carta.

Health and social care practice regularly requires decisions about both personal care and treatment, and also decisions about residence in a particular place for the purposes of receiving care and treatment. Prior to the advent of the Mental Capacity Act, when it was not possible to gain consent in relation to such decisions, there were two legal mechanisms which were used at different times in order to provide legal justification for related actions and ensure that people working in health and social care settings did not commit assault or battery or unlawfully deprive a person of liberty.

Until 1959, it was the doctrine of *parens patriae* which provided the legal basis for surrogate decision making on behalf of incapacitated adults (Szerletics, 2012). *Parens patriae* is a legal doctrine which gave both the power and the duty to the state or Crown to protect both the property and the personal welfare of vulnerable individuals (specifically children and those of unsound mind). While it largely developed as a means of administering financial affairs, it was regularly used to deal with issues relating to welfare, particularly for those deemed mentally ill.

The introduction of the 1959 Mental Health Act and the abolition of the royal warrant which provided the *parens patriae* legal power both took place in November 1960. After that time it was assumed that the statute of the Mental Health Act and the body of legal opinion in the Court of Protection would provide clear legal guidance in relation to matters relating to those diagnosed with mental illness. However, while the Court of Protection gained powers to deal with the financial matters of such persons, it had no powers to make decisions relating to care or personal welfare. Similarly, the new Mental Health Act obviously had provisions relating to mental illness and also provisions relating to property and affairs but none relating to questions of personal welfare – for example, what to do in the case of questions about the treatment of physical illness in a mentally ill person.

Since then, the notion of the 'doctrine of necessity' provided an alternative legal defence to that of informed consent or of *parens patriae*. In English law this doctrine has been cited in a range of cases since the mid-eighteenth century relating to the detention of those deemed a risk to themselves or others, where the detention could be shown to be 'necessary'. It has also been cited regularly in relation to medical treatments, particularly – for example, in relation to forced sterilisations. Under the common law doctrine of necessity, care or treatment may be administered to a mentally incapacitated adult, and 'reasonable' force may be used to do so, provided it is in the person's best interests.

The principle of necessity requires two things. First, that there must be a necessity to act when it is not practicable to communicate with the assisted person (for example, because of mental incapacity); and, second, that *the action taken must be such that a reasonable person would in all the circumstances take, acting in the best interests of the assisted person (Re F (Mental Patient: Sterilisation)* [1990]).

Research Summary 3.2

Significant case law

Three English court judgments between 1990 and 2013 illustrate some of the evolution of legal thinking in relation to issues of capacity and best interests.

A key case in 1990 related to a 36-year-old female with learning difficulties who had been judged to have the mental age of a small child. While resident in hospital she formed a sexual relationship with a male patient, and the hospital staff, after considering various options, suggested that F should be sterilised. The family supported the decision but could not make it on F's behalf. The mother applied to the court for a decision in relation to sterilisation, in F's best interests (*Re F (Mental Patient: Sterilisation)* [1990]). The court decided that it would be lawful for the doctors to operate on F without her consent.

Comments from the judge, Lord Goff, included the following:

We are searching for a principle upon which, in limited circumstances, recognition may be given to a need, in the interests of the patient, that treatment should be given to him in circumstances where he is (temporarily or permanently) disabled from consenting to it. It is this criterion of a need which points to the principle of necessity as providing justification.

We see here the notion of best interests, as well as that of necessity being referred to. This case was also important in highlighting the importance of the Bolam test in deciding whether a course of intervention is in a person's best interests. The Bolam test was introduced in 1957 in the process of determining certain issues relation to medical negligence. This test suggests that

'a doctor is not guilty of negligence if he has acted in accordance with a practice accepted as proper by a responsible body of medical men skilled in that particular form of treatment; nor is he negligent merely because there is a body of opinion which would adopt a different technique'.

(*Bolam v Friern Hospital Management Committee* [1957])

Since the Bolam test gives a narrowly medical view of best interests, it is unlikely that the same judgment would be made today.

(*Continued*)

(Continued)

In *Re Y* [1996], the court was asked to decide whether it was in the best interests of a severely learning disabled woman to donate her bone marrow to her seriously ill sister. The woman (Y) lacked the capacity to consent or refuse. The court considered the following factors in deciding whether it was in her best interests to donate the bone marrow.

Benefits

- Y would continue to benefit from contact with her family, consisting of visits to her residential home and involvement in family events outside the home.
- Her mother would continue to be able to visit her. The visits were important to Y, and they might reduce significantly if her sister became more seriously ill.
- Her sister was more likely to recover if she received bone marrow from Y, as opposed to from an unrelated donor. Although her sister's best interests were not the issue, her survival was in Y's best interests.
- Her mother and her sister would both be grateful to her, and she would benefit from this gratitude.

Disbenefits

- General anaesthesia carries some risks, but this did not appear to be any greater for Y than for anyone else in the population. Y would, in any event, be carefully monitored.
- Any anxieties that Y may have could be managed by a family member going with her to the operating theatre.
- Any pain could be managed by the administration of morphine.

In this case, the social and welfare benefits were considered to outweigh the medical and emotional disbenefits to Y, and permission was granted.

Since that time the balance-sheet approach, of weighing up benefits and disbenefits, and including emotional and family issues as well as purely medical ones, has become more widespread when the courts are trying to determine what is in the best interests of a person who lacks the capacity to make that determination for themselves. Such an approach is also recommended for professionals in order to assist and to document their practice (see Chapter 5).

A third case illustrates the evolution and current state of legal thinking in relation to best interests decision making.

Aintree University Hospitals NHS Foundation Trust v James is a case which reached the Supreme Court in 2013. This was the first time that the court was asked to make a judgment in relation to the MCA. The hospital concerned asked for a declaration under the Mental Capacity Act 2005 that it would be in the best interests of the patient, J, to have certain painful treatments withheld from him in the event of a significant deterioration in his condition.

One particularly important point to take from this judgment of the Supreme Court relates to best interests. The judges ruled that the court of Appeal had been wrong to use an objective test to determine what a patient would think rather than the subjective test used by the original trial judge. One of the judges emphasised that *the purpose of the best interests test is to consider the matters from the person's point of view* (Aintree University Hospitals NHS Foundation Trust v James [2013].

Comment

The cases above span almost a 25-year period and illustrate the evolution of thinking in relation to the notion of 'best interests' when considering vulnerable individuals. From an era in which the views of a body of medical men were seen as the last word in determining 'best interests', we have moved to the use of a balance-sheet approach which involves a much more holistic process and the consideration of many other factors relating to quality of life and individual preferences, as well as narrowly clinical or medical factors.

Where there have not been clear statute laws which could be applied, the doctrine of necessity has been invoked in many other scenarios in health and social care to justify decision making, including those requiring deprivation of liberty or residence in a particular place for the purposes of care and treatment.

Mental health legislation in the UK (currently, the Mental Health Act 1983, as amended 2007 in England) provides a clear and robust legal framework and a range of safeguards for those who come under its jurisdiction. For a long time it has been common for some individuals to be admitted to psychiatric hospitals 'informally', meaning that they are not subjected to legal detention under any section of the Mental Health Act. This process avoids forced detention and is often seen as fitting well with one of the principles in the *Code of Practice* which guides practitioners in applying the Act, namely that of looking for the least restrictive option (Department of Health, 2008b).

Many practitioners within health and social care and the legal professions have seen this as a satisfactory arrangement. In the original court judgment in the seminal Bournewood case, one of the judges described the adequacy of the doctrine of necessity, in relation to 'informal' patients, as follows:

> It was plainly the statutory intention that such patients would indeed be cared for, and receive such treatment for their condition as might be prescribed for them in their best interests. Moreover the doctors in charge would, of course, owe a duty of care to such a patient in their care. Such treatment and care can, in my opinion, be justified on the basis of the common law doctrine of necessity.
>
> (R v Bournewood Community and Mental Health
> NHS Trust ex parte L [1998])

Much more will be said in Chapter 6 about the seminal Bournewood case. For now, it should be noted that while there were dissenting voices at the time, there was a large body of opinion that supported the idea that the doctrine of necessity was sufficient to provide legal justification for the provision of care and treatment within settings of confinement. The culture of opinion has shifted significantly since then.

Filling the legal gap

In situations in which individuals are unable to make decisions for themselves and it is necessary to make those decisions, there are a number of options open in terms of frameworks to assist relevant decision makers and the courts in the process. Substituted judgment, best interests and advance decisions are all methods which are widely used in different settings and circumstances. Most jurisdictions consider that the principle of autonomy should be paramount, so that where possible the individual should always make their own decisions. For this reason advance directives are given primacy in most places, acknowledging the will of the person, as expressed when they had the capacity to do so. After that, some countries give precedence to the substituted judgment principle and others to best interests. We will consider each in turn.

Substituted judgment

Some jurisdictions, including the USA, use substituted judgment as the main basis for making decisions on behalf of those unable to make their own decisions. The term refers to the notion of making, as far as possible, the decision that the person themselves would have made if they were competent to do so. Note that this may not be the same as the decision that professionals or family members think might be best. However, it comes closest to preserving the principle of autonomy as surrogate decision makers and actors attempt to carefully decide on and do what the person would choose.

There are a number of difficulties inherent in this process. The first that might spring to mind is that while many people lose capacity after a period of being a competent adult (in the case of a brain injury, for example, or as Alzheimer's disease progresses), there are equally many who may have never had decisional capacity (those with severe learning disabilities, for example). This means that it is inherently difficult, if not impossible, to determine the decision that such a person would wish to make for themselves in any circumstance.

A well-known case from the USA illustrates this point. A 67-year-old man with severe learning difficulties who had spent most of his life in an institution developed leukaemia. A court was asked to decide whether chemotherapy should be tried as a treatment. A court-appointed guardian made a powerful argument that Mr Saikewicz should not receive treatment, based on the notion that he would experience a significant level of distress and pain from the treatment, and that this is what he himself would say were he able to express himself (Shalock et al., 2002, p34). Critics noted at the time that it is impossible to determine the decision that a person who has never been competent and never expressed a view would make.

Substituted judgment has also been a significant feature of English law at times, particularly in relation to issues of mental illness (Harmon, 1990). The 1959 Mental Health Act was referred to earlier. This statute brought in, from November 1960, the use of substituted judgment in English courts. Where people were mentally disordered and courts were asked to make judgments about their property and affairs, the court was asked to imagine that the person had a brief lucid interval in which they would make sane and rational decisions. This process led to what has been described as 'the high water mark of artificiality' in the case *Re C* (Szerletics, 2012). This was the kind of problematic case suggested earlier, in which it was not possible to determine the preferences of the person because they had never had capacity before. Here the court was asked to assume that the patient would have been 'a normal decent person, acting in accordance with contemporary standards of morality'. This is clearly artificial because it is imposing the standards of one group of people at a particular time on a person with no evidence that they might share such views, and is creating a false scenario by assuming, again with no evidence, how a person might behave in an imagined lucid interval.

Even in situations in which a person has had capacity in the past, it is by no means easy or certain to determine what that individual might do in the current situation which may be very different from any that they experienced when fully capacitous. The Mental Capacity Act rightly gives a good deal of weight to ascertaining a person's wishes and feelings as far as possible. It would be helpful if a person expressed very clearly what they might wish to happen in particular circumstances should they lose capacity, but this is not commonly the case, unless they have formally made an advance statement (see Chapters 4 and 6 for more information about advance decisions). The Mental Capacity Act makes it clear that the wishes and feelings of the person are important factors to consider but are not the only factor and are not necessarily the determining factors in arriving at a judgment about a course of action.

A further problem with the substituted judgment approach to decision making is the potential for abuse. A decision maker may state that the views which they are expressing are those of the person without capacity, but this may be a smoke screen for forwarding their own views and furthering only their own interests rather than those of the person lacking capacity.

Researchers in jurisdictions which continue to use substituted judgment widely have questioned whether it is a suitable method. For example, in the USA, Torke et al. (2008), after reviewing the evidence, suggested that *Given compelling evidence that the use of substituted judgment has insurmountable flaws, other approaches should be considered. One approach provides limits on decision making using a best interest standard based on community norms.*

During the lengthy debate and evidence-gathering process which preceded the Mental Capacity Act 2005, policy and law makers came to the same conclusion.

The evolution of 'best interests' decision making

In the first consultation which the Law Commission carried out in the development of the MCA, it noted the two distinct approaches which were offered by best interests and substituted judgment. The first was seen as more paternalistic and restrictive, since it is based on what the decision maker thinks objectively best for the patient. Recognising the problems and limitations of substituted judgment, the Commission recommended a best interests approach but one which should be blended with other approaches so that some attempt should be made by the decision maker to first go through a substituted judgment process and attempt to ascertain what the person themselves might decide. When the MCA finally arrived, both elements were maintained, and although it is abundantly clear that best interests provides the major framework which decision makers should follow, they are also encouraged to consider substituted judgment in the sense of trying to establish what the person may have decided by trying to ascertain any wishes and feelings which they may have expressed.

Social work practitioners are particularly aware of and sensitive to the dominance of the 'medical model' in many areas of practice. It is interesting to note that the notion of 'best interests' was for a long time one which was also highly aligned with a medical model. Both the legal and medical professions followed a consensus that a person's best interests equated with medical best interests, so that what the doctor deemed to be most appropriate medically was automatically assumed to determine best interests.

Legal decision makers were encouraged in this approach by the Bolam test, which seemed to give primacy to the views of a 'responsible body of medical men' (see Significant case law, page 31). This may have been appropriate when determining matters of medical negligence which were to do with just the actions of medical practitioners, but was less so when the same test was applied to many other health and social care decisions, often involving a multidisciplinary team and specific decisions which were more properly the remit of non-medical practitioners. Social workers may agree with the court, which suggested in 1994 that *there should not be a belief that what the doctor says is the patient's best interest is the patient's best interest (Frenchay Healthcare NHS Trust v S* [1994]). However, for some time courts continued to follow expert medical opinion when arriving at welfare decisions. Problems with this approach occurred when, for example, there was more than one body of expert medical opinion. By the beginning of the new century, a different approach was increasingly adopted, foreshadowing the process which was formalised in the Mental Capacity Act. We see, for example, in the case of *Re SL*, the judgment of LJ Butler-Sloss that *broader ethical, social, moral and welfare considerations including the invasive character of the proposed treatment' should be taken into account when trying to determine what course of action is objectively in a persons best interests (Re SL (Adult Patient) (Medical Treatment)).*

It was hoped that the MCA would put paid to the culture of defaulting to a medical opinion regardless of whether this is the most appropriate opinion to seek. However, as a comprehensive investigation by the House of Lords made clear, the culture of deference to and dominance of medical decision makers has continued in many settings (House of Lords, 2014).

Readers of this text are unlikely to need reminding of the need for a more holistic approach to best interests decision making. It is likely that your challenge is more likely to involve concerns of how to question the decision making of others which appears to be too medically focused. Here, reminding others of their legal obligations under the MCA, and seeking wider discussion and debate, may be useful. See Chapter 5 for more guidance on best interests meetings.

It is easy to say that the consideration of what constitutes best interests should be holistic and that decision makers should follow the checklist provided in the MCA. However, it remains complex and difficult to define in practice. This has led some to call for a clearer definition of best interests. But, as one judge noted, *the infinite variety of the human condition never ceases to surprise and it is that fact that defeats any attempt to be more precise in a definition of best interests (Portsmouth NHS Trust v Wyatt & Ors* [2004]).

It should be noted that while 'substituted judgment' and 'best interests' are two clearly different approaches conceptually and in practice, there are areas of overlap and, as the courts have noted on more than one occasion, where there are no countervailing factors, the two may have been deemed equivalent by the courts.

The above provides a comparative overview of how we arrived at the dominance of the 'best interests' principle within our legislative framework. More information about the details and implementation of best interests decision making can be found in Chapter 5.

Who is the decision maker?

One of the notable differences between the framework enacted in the MCA and that used in many other countries is that here the identity of the decision maker is entirely dependent on the nature of the health or welfare decision (Dunn et al., 2007). Many other countries adopt a guardianship approach in which responsibility for a whole range of different decisions is given to one substitute decision maker who is appointed as a guardian. The MCA provides that the decision maker should be the person most relevant to and involved in the course of action proposed. This often leads to confusion in practice and the issue is discussed in more detail in Chapters 4 and 5. At this point note that, as a social worker, the kinds of decisions for which you are most likely to be identified as the decision maker relate to change of accommodation, such as the move into a residential care home or supported housing.

United Nations Convention on the Rights of Persons with Disabilities

Much of the literature relating to rights-based approaches to working with people with impairments or disabilities focuses on the Human Rights Act in terms of a legislative framework. This remains the most important piece of relevant law but it should be noted that, since 2006, the United Nations has adopted a Convention on the Rights of Persons with Disabilities. Courts have on a number of occasions referred to this framework when making judgments in relation to cases brought by persons with disabilities (Equality and Human Rights Commission, 2010).

Article 12 of this Convention has particular significance. It provides the right to equal recognition before the law, and guidance from the EHRC makes it clear what this should mean in relation to decision making. It explains that *this means that disabled people cannot be denied the right to make their own decisions. If they need help to make decisions then this should be given* (Equality and Human Rights Commission, 2010). This provides further legal emphasis and backing for the principles and duties which personalisation, the Care Act and the MCA have introduced into health and social care practice.

Adult safeguarding

The discussion so far in this chapter has focused on decision making in situations in which a person is assessed as lacking the capacity to make that decision for themselves. Much of social work involves working with vulnerable people who do have the capacity to make their own decisions. This brings a separate set of dilemmas and challenges and it seems that there can be particular problems when issues of vulnerability and capacity are conflated or confused.

In terms of adult safeguarding, it had been thought for some years that the law was not sufficiently robust to provide the required protection and remedies in relation to work with vulnerable adults. The Care Act 2014 has strengthened the law in many respects.

The Act has introduced six principles which should underpin all adult safeguarding work. Please refer to Chapter 7 for more detailed information about working with vulnerable adults. Here, we would emphasise two points. First, the Care Act is clear about the principles which should underpin decision making when working with any vulnerable adult.

The second point is that, despite such a clear framework of principles, decision making in this area is often difficult and complex because of the need to take into account the views of a range of different people who may have differing and conflicting opinions, and because of the tension between the imperative to protect and safeguard clashing with the imperative to empower and allow people to make their own decisions.

It can be tricky to work out what to do when faced with such dilemmas. It has been noted that social workers in adult social care are at times unclear about their legal responsibilities, powers and constraints (Preston-Shoot and Wrigley, 2002). A clear understanding of the relevant legal frameworks will not provide all the answers, but will certainly help to make for more appropriate decision making.

Examples of how not to approach this issue may also help to inform consideration of how to approach decision making in this complex area.

There have been a number of documented cases in which vulnerable adults have been left at risk of harm, in some cases leading to their deaths, after disengaging from services in a way which was not questioned by social workers. When asked about their conduct in such cases, and whether the individuals concerned had the mental capacity to make such decisions, social workers regularly referred to the statutory *presumption of capacity* (House of Lords, 2014).

You will find further discussion in Chapter 4 about the MCA and about capacity assessments.

Clearly, it is necessary and should be possible to ally an approach which involves people and empowers independent decision making with one which maintains a sensible scrutiny of their capabilities and vulnerabilities.

Beyond the individual social worker, there is worrying evidence that local authorities at times use presumption of capacity to avoid taking responsibility for a vulnerable person. The Law Society has reported *lots of cases where a person has been neglecting themselves and the local authority or relevant health agency has used the presumption of capacity to allow that to continue* (House of Lords, 2014). As it suggests, it is a *perverse use of the Mental Capacity Act to use the assumption of capacity as a way of avoiding assessing it*. Other bodies reporting on the same issue were more stark and cynical in their analysis of the issue. If you work within a local authority and are aware of this happening, the reasoning and decision making should be challenged and discussed. It can be helpful to discuss things with your Legal Department.

Decision making and uncertainty

So far in this chapter we have largely discussed legislative frameworks and principles which are designed to uphold the rights of service users when professionals make decisions with them and about them. We have noted some of the legal debates and the gaps which exist between legal principles and the realities in practice. It is easy to suggest that such gaps can be filled with more and better training, but we must also recognise that, in reality, human decision making is often influenced very largely by unconscious factors.

There is a fairly significant body of work looking at decision making in social work. However, perhaps some of the most notable and useful work in relation to human decision making comes from the work of Tversky and Kahneman. Winners of a Nobel prize, their article 'Judgement under uncertainty: Heuristics and biases' has, for good reasons, become one of the most highly cited works in social science (Tversky and Kahneman, 1974).

Through a programme of psychological research over a number of years, the authors elucidated many of the mechanisms by which we take short cuts and use limited information to reach quick decisions. Much of the time this process will lead us to a correct judgement, which is why we often default to such 'quick' thinking. However, the heuristics or rules of thumb, and biases, which enable us to take short cuts to decision making, are such that they can also often lead us to erroneous conclusions.

The human brain has evolved to search for and recognise patterns, and this facility has enabled us to be hugely successful. However, it also means that we have a tendency to see patterns where none exist. This is perhaps one of the reasons that conspiracy theories are so popular. Also, authors such as Taleb (2001) have shown that randomness is far more common in life and in nature than we like to think, and because the drive to search for patterns and meaning is very strong, we often read patterns and meanings into situations where there are none, and also infer patterns based on previous experience, particularly if that experience is recent.

Kahneman (2012) describes two different systems the human brain uses for decision making, and describes the two different modes as 'fast' and 'slow' thinking. This idea of the two systems is also something of a heuristic. That is, rather than a strictly accurate description of how the brain operates, it gives a useful and concise overview of two very distinct ways in which we process and arrive at decisions.

System 1 refers to what is often described as intuitive decision making. This kind of mental operation is very good at integrating information about one subject but less so at dealing with multiple different topics at once. It is also not good at dealing with numerical/statistical information.

System 2 describes the kind of mental activity which is consciously deliberative, but which requires effort and attention. We tend to identify ourselves as conscious reasoning beings who make most of our decisions using this kind of deliberative process. However, it is literally true that we have a limited span of attention and can only process a limited amount of information at any one time in this deliberative way. The mental activity associated with this system requires focused attention and is disrupted when attention is drawn away. Thus, and as a significant body of research has shown, a much greater part of our mental processing and decision making is operated by System 1 than we are aware of.

Developing awareness of this can enable us to be more reflexive and to test assumptions and judgements more critically when important decisions are being made. Heuristics and short cuts can serve us well when there is real urgency and when we have sufficient expertise, but it is useful to take a step back and analyse information when possible.

Some of the more common heuristics and biases which have been noted in decision making research and which generally flow from what might be called System 1 decision making are listed below.

Availability and representativeness heuristics

This refers to tendencies to estimate the likelihood of an event by comparing it to examples of the event which can easily be brought to mind or by comparing it to a prototype or stereotype that we are familiar with. This can lead to major errors. The most recent or emotionally powerful example of something may be easy to recall and thus mentally easily 'available', but may have features which are quite different from the current situation. Comparing the example to a prototype or stereotype can be misleading for various reasons, particularly because it may ignore the base rate of a problem.

Consider the following description of Tara. She listens to a lot of New Age music and her house always smells of aromatherapy oils. In her spare time she studies homoeopathy and astrology. Is Tara more likely to be an aromatherapist or a school teacher? Many people suggest that she is more likely to be an aromatherapist because the behaviours described fit with our image and stereotype of what that kind of person might do. In fact, in terms of probability, she is much more likely to be a school teacher. There are some 400,000 teachers in the UK compared to no more than a few thousand aromatherapists. Because the 'base rate' of teachers is much higher, any individual is much more likely to be a teacher than an aromatherapist in terms of their main job, regardless of their characteristics.

Anchoring

The availability heuristic also links to the idea of 'anchoring'. A short cut to making a decision can be made by using a clear reference point or anchor which easily comes to mind. If a piece of information was recently brought to your attention it will affect the way you view subsequent pieces of information and the way that you make decisions. This effect is used all the time in sales. You are much more likely to buy an item that has been shown as on sale for £50 and is then reduced to £25 than if it were on sale the whole time at £25.

The effect can be used to persuade people to do useful things, too. In a 1975 study, people were asked whether they would volunteer for two hours per week for two years. All the respondents said no. When they were then asked whether they would volunteer for a single two-hour event, half said yes. Another group was asked to volunteer for the single event without first asking for the two-year commitment. From this group only 17 per cent said yes.

Anchoring is an apt word to describe this tendency. The initial information or value that we focus on will not only have a strong influence, but we tend not to change our minds so much in the light of new information once we have locked on or anchored to an initial judgement.

Confirmation bias

Another way of understanding that tendency to anchor to an initial judgement is to talk about 'confirmation bias'. The cliché that first impressions last has repeatedly been shown to be true. It saves mental work if we can make a rapid judgement and then filter subsequent information to fit with that judgement, and it is clear that our first, very rapid appraisal of a person influences how new information about the person is interpreted (Sutherland, 1992). It has been shown that this is a contributory factor to misdiagnosis and medical errors and it may be problematic for all decision making. Munro (2008) found that evidence given by children and junior staff was rejected if that evidence did not conform to the beliefs of the interviewer. At the point of taking a referral, a strongly worded though inaccurate statement about the mental capacity of a service user may influence your approach to working with them, however careful you are to make your own subsequent assessment. Can we overcome this bias? Not entirely, but it has been shown that experts and those who spend more time researching an area are less prone to the anchoring bias in decision making.

Fundamental attribution error

We should also note what has been termed the 'fundamental attribution error' by psychologists. What they mean by this is the tendency to attribute a person's behaviour to their personality, disposition or some internal characteristic, and to ignore or underplay the role of situational factors. It is noteworthy that people living in more individualistic cultures have been shown to be more prone to the error than those in more collectivist societies (Miller, 1984).

When considering whether a person's behaviour provides evidence of a lack of mental capacity, recognition of this common error should lead us to think carefully about the role of the environment and situational factors. (See Chapter 5 for further discussion about consideration of time and place when assessing mental capacity in relation to a decision.)

It is of no surprise that such short cuts and rules of thumb are often used by social workers who are faced with trying to make sense of complex evidence to arrive at a decision or series of decisions while under significant time and work pressures. There is also clear evidence that this leads at times to significant errors. This has been established in relation to child protection work (Munro, 1999) and work with vulnerable adults (Kirkman and Melrose, 2014).

When hurried and under pressure, we are more likely to act based on what happened with our last case or visit, or on other slightly similar cases, whether they are relevant or not.

Research Summary 3.3

In 2013 the UK government commissioned the behavioural insights team to conduct research about decision making by social workers (Kirkman and Melrose, 2014). While this research focused on front-line child protection social work, many of the findings have equal relevance for work with adults.

The researchers confirmed the points noted above in the decision-making literature and found the following.

Time and workload pressures increase the reliance upon social workers' intuition to make decisions.

A range of behavioural biases affect social workers' ability to make objective judgements. These include, for example, the availability heuristic (people make judgements about the probability of events based on how easy it is to think of examples), confirmation bias (only looking for evidence that confirms pre-existing views) and the tendency to judge cases on their relative rather than objective merits.

The complexity of social workers' decision making is increased further by the fact that many sequential decisions have to be made through the course of a single day, which engenders depletion or 'decision fatigue'.

One recommendation was that the rules of thumb or heuristics which are effective in assisting professionals in making fast decisions are incorporated into decision tools.

Another recommendation was that feedback loops are used more widely and consciously to learn from experience.

Comment

You may have little control over time and workload pressures. However, being proactive in the use of supervision, prioritising some time for reflection and using appropriate decision tools may all assist in ensuring more sound decision making. See also Becoming a social worker, below.

Becoming a social worker

What Kahneman refers to as fast, or intuitive, thinking is informed by two clear processes. One involves expertise and the rapid processing of information based on significant previous experience. This is more likely to lead to an appropriate solution or answer to a question. In the absence of such experience our brain will use heuristics and biases which may be more likely to give us incorrect answers.

If fast thinking does not provide us with a clear judgement, or if we know that we are lacking in relevant experience and our immediate judgements may be subject to inappropriate heuristics and biases, it is all the more important to use 'slow' thinking and use reasoning and detailed analysis to arrive at a solution.

This reinforces the importance of taking the time, as someone new to a role, to think through options, verbalise them, write them down, and use supervision and the expertise of colleagues who do have experience, to assist you in arriving at sound judgements. This is the process through which, over time, you will be able to become more adept at making decisions based on appropriate fast thinking based on professional expertise.

Fook et al. (2000) suggest that 'novices' are more likely to follow rules and experts are more likely to follow a 'critically reflective process'. When relatively inexperienced and uncertain, rules and tools may provide a useful steer. However, they should not be used uncritically and their value should be assessed in each case, and on reflection in the light of the outcomes of their use.

The feedback loops recommended by Kirkman and Melrose (2014) are an important element in ensuring that experience is actually useful in facilitating relevant learning. This reinforces the importance of carefully assessing not only your input into a case but also the outcomes. Reviewing cases with colleagues and/or in supervision provides an important vehicle for this process.

As well as reviewing individual cases from your own agency and practice, a very useful way of learning from the more general experience of your profession is to read reports which review individual or collections of cases and make recommendations based on those reviews. We suggest that two contrasting types of literature may be helpful in this regard.

First, serious case reviews provide very useful learning about what went wrong and why, in cases in which services are seen to have failed and a service user has come to harm as a result.

Second, good practice guidelines and examples highlight the kind of practice which works well and offer analysis of why that practice may lead to good outcomes. The Social Care Institute for Excellence (SCIE) website is a good starting point for such examples (see www.scie.org.uk).

Chapter Summary

The foregoing has highlighted some elements of the debate with regard to decision making on behalf of those who lack capacity as it developed over the decades. It is clear that after lengthy deliberation, both health and social care professionals and legal professionals generally agreed that the 'best interests' principle and method, while not perfect in many respects, is the best method overall for arriving at a judgement. The next two chapters provide more detail on the ways in which the Mental Capacity Act enshrines and gives primacy to the 'best interests' principle, and some of the challenges and dilemmas of putting this into practice.

As well as highlighting the evolution of relevant legal frameworks and the best interests principle, the chapter has also highlighted some key aspects of decision making in professional practice. Some of the things which guide and influence the decision making of social workers were considered, along with some of the problems that occur when relying on mental short cuts and when making decisions too quickly that require more time for deliberation.

The tension between the imperative to empower and the imperative to protect will always remain a significant challenge for social work practice. A sound understanding of relevant legislation, of the psychology of human decision making and of tools which can help the process, can help in navigating this difficult area and ensuring that you reach justified and appropriate decisions.

We hope that the case studies and material featured in this chapter and throughout the book begin to clarify and address the ways in which we should be using legal frameworks and other tools to approach decision making and working with vulnerable adults. Please see the links to further resources below and at the ends of other chapters for further guidance.

Further Reading

House of Lords Select Committee on the Mental Capacity Act 2005 (2014) *Mental Capacity Act 2005: Post-Legislative Scrutiny.* London: The Stationery Office.

This detailed report is worth scrutinising in detail as it provides a very useful overview of the kind of decision making which takes place across a range of health and social care settings in relation to vulnerable adults. Examples of both very good and very poor practice are scrutinised, and a number of sound recommendations emerge. Equally, the government response to this document gives a good overview of the kind of legal and policy responses which are likely to emerge in the next few years.

Kahneman, D (2012) *Thinking Fast and Slow.* London: Penguin.

This is a very approachable overview of what decades of psychological research have taught us about human decision making. While not specific to social work, it provides one of the best texts for understanding the factors that influence how any human being may make decisions in the real world.

Chapter 4

Mental capacity

Meeting professional standards

This chapter will help you to develop the following selected capabilities, to the appropriate level, from the social work Professional Capabilities Framework.

Diversity

- Recognise oppression and discrimination by individuals or organisations and implement appropriate strategies to challenge.

Rights, justice and economic well-being

- Address oppression and discrimination, applying the law to protect and advance people's rights, recognising how legislation can constrain or advance these rights.
- Apply in practice principles of human, civil rights and equalities legislation, and manage competing rights, differing needs and perspectives.

Knowledge

- Demonstrate knowledge and application of appropriate legal and policy frameworks and guidance that inform and mandate social work practice.
- Apply legal reasoning, using professional legal expertise and advice appropriately, recognising where scope for professional judgement exists.
- Understand forms of harm and their impact on people, and the implications for practice, drawing on concepts of strength, resilience, vulnerability, risk and resistance, and apply to practice.

Intervention and skills

- Demonstrate clear communication of evidence-based professional reasoning, judgements and decisions, to professional and non-professional audiences.

Implementation is improving, but we still have a very long way to go. Many workers can recite the principles, but try to ask them how these translate into everyday practice, and they struggle to answer.

(House of Lords, 2013b, p915)

Introduction

In this chapter we will explore the use of the Mental Capacity Act 2005 when working with adults who may be at risk. In particular, we wish to focus on key aspects of the legislation and how they relate to day-to-day social work practice. Promoters of the MCA make the case that it is a *visionary piece of legislation* placing *the individual at the heart of decision making* (House of Lords, 2013a, p8), but the application of the law can present practitioners with as many dilemmas as it aims to resolve. As the quote above indicates, training has gone some way to embedding a knowledge of the principles but understanding clearly how to implement those principles remains a challenge for many practitioners. We hope to provide some useful guidance in relation to this, but before we address practice issues we will provide a brief summary as to how and why the MCA came into force.

The need for the Act

The legislation is a product of more than 15 years' work and the need for it was first highlighted by the Law Society in 1989 when it published a paper entitled *Decision Making and Mental Incapacity*. This then led to the involvement of the Law Commission in 1991, which produced a consultation paper, *Mentally Incapacitated Adults and Decision-making*. The paper stated the following:

> *The existing law relating to decision making on behalf of mentally incapacitated adults is fragmented, complex and in many respects out of date. There is no coherent concept of their status and there are many gaps where the law provides no effective mechanism for resolving problems.*

(Law Commission, 1991, para. 1.9)

Significant gaps highlighted by the Law Commission's report included clear legal guidance in relation to the following.

1. Consent to medical treatment.

2. Disputes between relatives.

3. Significant life decisions such as where to live.

4. Suspicions of abuse and neglect – who should intervene and be responsible for the decisions.

5. Young people leaving care – who has responsibility for making decisions on their behalf if they are unable to do so.

It is worth noting that before the MCA social workers and other professionals were often working in legal limbo. There were some provisions for those judged to lack capacity to handle their financial affairs under the Mental Health Act 1983 and the original Court of Protection, but otherwise there was little legal guidance as to how to intervene in service users' lives and make decisions on their behalf. Historically, decisions for adults who lacked capacity were generally made in consultation with family and/or other professionals, while attempts were made by social workers to empower and/or verbally persuade service users to agree to a certain plan of action. Brown and Barber (2008) helpfully identify some of the tensions which resulted from such practice:

> Another issue is how to identify an acceptable level of risk for an individual. If a professional intervenes without a clear legal base and guidance, they lay themselves open to allegations of undue influence or misconduct. If they do not intervene, they may be accused of neglecting their duty of care.

(p2)

The MCA has now provided us with a legal framework, but it includes the principle that individuals are allowed to make unwise decisions and this can often seem to conflict with services' perception of their duty to protect individuals from coming to harm. We explore this tension later in this chapter and also in more detail in the chapter on best interests. This principle was included in a statement of principles, following the scrutiny of a draft Mental Incapacity Bill (2003) by a Joint Committee of the Houses of Parliament. Other significant changes at this stage included the change of title from 'Incapacity' to 'Capacity', changes to the proposals for Lasting Powers of Attorney and an addition of standards of professional conduct which are included in the *Code of Practice* (see Further Reading). Thus, the Mental Capacity Act came into being with a clear emphasis on promoting the concept of capacity and with a statement of principles that should guide our actions when applying this law.

The five statutory principles

The five statutory principles are set out right at the beginning of the Mental Capacity Act in section 1 and before the definition of lack of capacity. The fact that they are incorporated into the legislation as opposed to the *Code of Practice* is an indication of the emphasis that the drafters wished to place on these. The principles are as follows.

- A person must be assumed to have capacity unless it is established that he lacks capacity.

- A person is not to be treated as unable to make a decision unless all practicable steps to help him do so have been taken without success.

- A person is not to be treated as unable to make a decision merely because he makes an unwise decision.

- An act done, or a decision made, under the act on behalf of a person who lacks capacity must be done, or made, in best interests.

- Before the act is done, or the decision is made, regard must be had to whether the purpose for which it is needed can be effectively achieved in a way that is less restrictive of the person's rights and freedom of action.

As a social worker, you may feel that these statements reflect your wish to empower individuals and to respect their rights and autonomy, but it is worth remembering that the law applies to any number of professionals or workers who come across vulnerable people in their day-to-day work. For example, police officers or paramedics may not be so familiar with such a value base and you may need to promote these principles when working with other agencies. Jones (2012) points out that a change of attitudes will be necessary to apply the law as it was intended:

> There can be no doubt that The Mental Capacity Act represents a major advance in that it provides a comprehensive statutory framework … However, the framework could prove to be an empty vessel if not 'accompanied by changes in attitude which recognise the rights of those lacking capacity and the need to instil respect and good practice in dealing with them'.

> (Joint Committee, 2003, p9)

Putting principles into practice

The Mental Capacity Act was passed in 2005 and came into force in England and Wales in 2007. Despite the fact that it has been in force for seven years, there is still a degree of ignorance and lack of clarity among workers around who should be using it and when.

A review undertaken by the House of Lords in 2013–14 as part of 'post-legislative scrutiny' reviewed a great deal of evidence. Submissions included the following comments in relation to a question as to whether the core principles of the Act are appropriate:

> The principles of the MCA are laudable, but in our experience can be used as an excuse to do nothing (I have presumed capacity so need take no action); can paralyse workers (is it an unwise decision and if so, what do we do to 'protect' someone); create confusion as to whose best interests are we really meeting, the person or their family? The principles are appropriate, but need to be better understood by everyone.

> (House of Lords, 2013b, p914)

How as a social worker can you ensure that the law does not become an 'empty vessel' and that you are not paralysed into inaction? We will explore these issues by means of the two main case studies running through the book, and other relevant cases, focusing on principles 1, 2 and 3 as well as the implications of the two-stage test for capacity. We will address principles 4 and 5 in the next two chapters. This is a useful point to also pause and rewind, and revisit the discussions in Chapter 2 in relation to the role of values and principles, whether enshrined in law, policy, professional codes or otherwise.

Principle 1 – The assumption of capacity

In relation to the first principle, it has become evident that many practitioners are hearing the message about 'assuming capacity' but not paying heed to the corollary 'unless established otherwise'. The result is that, instead of taking any clues that a person may lack capacity as the cue for a possible formal assessment of capacity, in many cases capacity is simply assumed even where there is clear evidence to the contrary. As Kirsty Keywood put it, *there is something about the presumption of capacity as it is currently worded in the Mental Capacity Act that has obscured the thinking of a number of people working at the grass roots* (House of Lords, 2013b, p908).

Evidence submitted to the Lords Committee suggested that some of this may be motivated by a misguided sense that labelling a person as incapacitated is somehow discriminatory and therefore inappropriate. They heard the following evidence:

> In their efforts to be non discriminatory, the social worker did not want to say the person met the first part of the two-stage test and had an impairment of the mind or brain: this led to them not having a capacity assessment, although this was later rectified following reflective discussion. However, this is not a 'one off' happening and many more people may not be having their capacity assessed due to the good intentions of workers.

(House of Lords, 2013b, p938)

Social work values rightly focus on empowerment of individuals and the avoidance of discriminatory practice. However, sound assessment skills are an equally important part of the social work toolkit and unless we assess clearly and identify things accurately we are in danger of leaving vulnerable service users at risk. If a person is truly lacking capacity in relation to a decision and we fail to assess this, then the person is at risk of not receiving all the protections and empowerment which the Mental Capacity Act affords.

Principle 2 – Taking all practicable steps to help a person make a decision

Principle 3 – Unwise decisions

Case Study 4.1

Consider these issues in relation to Rosemary Cave (see pages 4–6). As you will recall, you have arrived on the ward to assess Rosemary and have just been intercepted by her estranged daughter, asking questions. You now take time to interview Rosemary.

Rosemary seems glad to have your company; she talks at length about her childhood home in Exeter and her recollection of the war and air raids. Rosemary is insistent that she needs to find her mother, because people are picking on her. Rosemary seems unaware that she is in hospital but is clear she needs to go home to her mother. You ask Rosemary how she likes it here and she replies that they are all 'interfering busybodies' and should leave her alone. Rosemary makes a grimace when you mention Mark's name, saying he is lazy; she does not respond when you ask her about her daughter. In a moment of clarity Rosemary says that she has always hated hospitals and needs to go back to Ash Gardens, her home address. Rosemary then starts crying for her mother again.

How can you enhance Rosemary's capacity to make her own decision?

Comment

Before attempting to answer this question, take a moment to consider the first two principles. The assumption that Rosemary has capacity to make her own decisions may prove difficult to maintain after this initial conversation and the temptation might be to proceed direct to a capacity assessment, but the second principle points to a pause in this process and guides you to take all practicable steps to enable Rosemary to make her own decisions.

Each service user you will meet will have a different set of needs (whether these are in relation to communication or understanding) and you will have to identify these in order to take the right steps to enable decision making. For example, if you were working with an individual with brain damage, you might need to consult with the relevant expert to establish which part of the person's brain had been injured and how this might affect their cognition and perception. The taking of 'all practicable steps' should involve you having some skills and knowledge in relation to particular client groups, but more importantly will depend on the time you make available for this. For those service users, such as Rosemary, who suffer from memory loss and disorientation, factors to consider are as follows:

- *Is there a time of day when Rosemary is more able to understand or retain information?*
- *Is there a better environment in which to assess Rosemary's capacity, consider comfort and noise levels?*
- *Does Rosemary have untreated medical conditions such as an ongoing urinary tract infection which, if treated, could improve her decision-making abilities?*
- *Is there a friend or family member who could assist in explaining Rosemary's health and social care needs to her and what the choices are?*
- *Are there different ways you could communicate with Rosemary to improve her understanding – for example, using a memory prompt board?*

Please refer to Chapter 3 of the Code of Practice *(see Further Reading) for helpful guidance on how people can be helped to make their own decisions.*

(Continued)

(Continued)

The House of Lords Committee (2014) stresses that the 'empowerment ethos' of the law has not been delivered and that there is little evidence to suggest that practitioners are taking the time to enable decision making, often as a result of time and resources being scarce:

> To assess, engage and empower a person who may lack capacity can be resource intensive. It may require help from speech therapists or occupational therapists or for more time to be devoted to that person by the care staff or clinical team supporting them.
>
> *(Evidence submitted by MIND, p41)*

As suggested above, you may need to involve others such as the nursing staff in order to clarify how to support Rosemary with her decision making and thus work out, for example, what is the best time of day for her. Jones (2012) points out that Although practicable steps must be taken to help a person make a decision those assisting the person must be aware of subjecting the person to undue influence *(p12). This is pertinent if you decide to use family members or friends to try to help someone make a decision with support and is sometimes referred to as 'relational capacity'. There are inherent risks in this approach especially if you do not know the nature of the relationship between the vulnerable adult and other person.*

Unwise decisions

Principle 3 enshrines the right of an individual to make an unwise decision. Clearly, we all make unwise decisions in our lives and it is often the outcome of these decisions which will dictate how we view them in hindsight, especially when they involve taking risks. For example, free climbing is a dangerous sport, but those who engage in it would not be assessed as lacking capacity unless they did not understand the risks involved. As a social worker you have a duty to allow your service users to make unwise decisions, but when do unwise or irrational decisions lead us to suspect that an individual is lacking capacity? This question can become further complicated when there are safeguarding aspects to a case and anxiety levels are heightened with regard to the duty to protect adults at risk.

Jones (2012) highlights that courts have cited an irrational decision as evidence of lack of capacity, and goes on to quote from the case (*D v R (the Deputy of S) and S* [2010]) where the judge comments: *the fact that a decision is unwise or foolish may not, without more, be treated as conclusive, but it remains … a relevant consideration for the court to take into account in considering whether the criteria of inability to make a decision for oneself … are satisfied* (p14). Perhaps more helpfully this judge goes on to emphasise that unwise decisions need to be considered within the context of how an individual might have made a similar decision previously. For example, the decision of a Jehovah's Witness to refuse a blood transfusion may puzzle and disconcert those wishing to give treatment, but this decision could be argued to be consistent with that person's belief system and part of the cultural norm for that group. Whereas when an older person with memory loss starts to give their money away or spends erratically, this could prove to be a more difficult area to assess capacity for.

Case Study 4.2

Take a moment to think about Carl and his wish to live independently (see pages 6–7). Whose responsibility is it if this proves to be an unwise decision?

Comment

The simple answer to this is that it is Carl's responsibility. As the social worker involved, however, you have some responsibility in terms of any capacity assessment you make and the conclusion you reach around Carl having capacity, but this is potentially an unwise decision. Provided you have documentation of your reasons for reaching such a conclusion, it is hard to envisage how you could be held responsible for any untoward outcomes.

Decisions that you take as a social worker when assuming capacity or allowing one of your service users to make an unwise decision will depend on how you interpret or weigh the information available to you. This weighing and interpretation will clearly be guided by your values and it is possible that these values may conflict with others involved in a person's care, particularly if the person may come to harm as a result of an unwise decision. Different professionals and workers may interpret the law differently:

> Laws do not tell us what we ought to do, just what we can do ... Most decisions in social work involve a complex interaction of ethical, political, technical and legal issues, all of which are interconnected. Our values will influence how we interpret the law.

(Banks, 2012, p18)

Those involved in relationships where they experience domestic abuse and maybe choose after a period of separation to return to an abusive partner can challenge our notion of what is the 'right decision', but if this person also has a history of mental health difficulties or a learning disability, the contention about what is an incapacitated decision and what is an unwise decision can become more heated. One worker might interpret the fact that the individual is vulnerable as a consequence of their mental health or learning disability and therefore argue the case for incapacity and the need to intervene in best interests; another might argue that this is an unwise decision the person should be allowed to make. How such debates are resolved is usually through a series of capacity assessments and at times obtaining second opinions. The Court of Protection can also be approached if necessary for a declaration on capacity. The House of Lords Committee report (2013a) is clear that professional cultures can be averse to allowing individuals to make unwise decisions: *The concept of unwise decision making faces institutional obstruction due to the prevailing cultures of risk-aversion and paternalism* (p8).

There have been a number of cases in the Court of Protection in recent years that have supported the right of vulnerable individuals to make unwise decisions. Some judges have identified that the strong professional impetus and motivation to protect may result in the bar being set too high for such individuals to be assessed as having capacity. While it is important to be aware of this trend, some of these cases have been around decisions to marry or to have sexual relations and these are not decisions covered by section 5 of the Act, which provides protection against liability for acts in relation to care and treatment. (Please refer to Chapter 6 of the *Code of Practice* (see Further Reading) for a list of decisions or acts that can be made in a person's best interests.)

> The plain fact is that anyone who has sat in the family jurisdiction for as long as I have, spends the greater part of their life dealing with the consequences of unwise decisions made in personal relationships. The intention of the Act is not to dress an incapacitous person in forensic cotton wool but to allow them as far as possible to make the same mistakes that all other human beings are at liberty to make and not infrequently do.
>
> (Justice Hedley, *An NHS Trust v P & anor* [2013], cited in Pitblado, 2013, p2)

The above quote may seem to challenge the duty you have as a social worker to safeguard vulnerable individuals, but it is important to remember that the Court of Protection is there to support you and other professionals, where there is genuine uncertainty or disagreement over whether a service user has capacity or not for a specific decision. The court may also help you as a social worker take positive risks in your practice and take decisions, where the potential outcomes for a vulnerable adult are life threatening. In a case concerning an older woman who was severely depressed at being in a care home and threatened to take her life if she remained there, but was equally at risk of coming to grave harm as a result of poorly controlled diabetes and a lack of a 24-hour care package if she returned home, the judge commented: *There are risks either way and it is perfectly appropriate that the responsibility for the outcome should fall on the shoulders of the Court and not on the shoulders of the parties* (Jackson, 2013).

Maintaining the balance between promoting autonomous decision making and protecting the vulnerable is never easy, and we must constantly weigh the competing factors and demands. Returning to the first principle of the Act and the point highlighted earlier, one of the most dangerous things that can happen when working with vulnerable adults is for the practitioner to overlook vulnerability and lack of capacity, assume capacity and then allow a person to make unwise decisions which lead to greater vulnerability and significant harm. As mentioned above in relation to Carl, the act of carrying out a capacity assessment is also your protection against liability.

In terms of ethics, one of the notable theoretical frameworks for ethics is the 'consequentialist' one. This suggests that whether an act is right or wrong depends on the consequences of that act (Beckett and Maynard, 2005, p38). This reminds us that we must think clearly about the possible outcomes of our decisions to intervene or not intervene. They say that 'hindsight has 20/20 vision' and we cannot often foresee or foretell all the consequences of our decisions and non-decisions. However, there is a plethora of risk assessment and decision-making tools to assist us in thinking through various scenarios when working with the vulnerable. Refer back to the discussions in Chapter 3 in relation to decision making – these are very pertinent to such debates.

It should be noted, of course, that those who favour other approaches to ethics may think through a situation differently. Those who favour virtue ethics may think that the action which accords most closely with social work values should be followed, though this still leaves the question of which among various competing values should be prioritised. Those who favour deontological principles might ask which course of action would fit best with universal principles and ethical rules (Banks, 2006, p7). In the latter case, the principle of self-determination might be privileged, for example, and this brings us back to the principles of the MCA which are framed around promoting self-determination as far as possible. Where this is not possible, we might argue that best interests is a sound universal principle to adopt.

They are extreme examples but the serious case reviews such as that relating to Steven Hoskin (see below) highlight some of these issues, and the consequences of not intervening when there are clues about significant vulnerability and lack of capacity which are not acted on.

Research Summary 4.1

Learning from serious case reviews

Steven Hoskin lived in a rural area of Cornwall. He was 39 years old at the time of his death. It became apparent in early childhood that he had a significant learning disability. He did not read and after leaving school at 16 he was unable to secure employment. He resided for 14 months in an NHS assessment and treatment unit. While there he was 'victimised' by other trainees. He was assessed for community services in 1993 and deemed to have 'substantial' needs according to FACS (fair access to care services) criteria. He was reassessed in 2003 and weekly visits were recommended. After 11 visits he discontinued care in 2005 and subsequently health records show a significant increase in his contact with services.

(Continued)

(Continued)

In the last days of his life Steven was harassed, bullied and tortured in his flat, after a group made unproven accusations that he was a paedophile. He was finally murdered by this gang, who pushed him off the St Austell railway viaduct where his body was found the next day. Three of the gang were ultimately prosecuted.

A significant decision point in this case was the time at which Steven disengaged with services. This decision was not questioned despite there being clear evidence that Steven was not capable of expressing free choices.

One of the recommendations from the resulting serious case review was that the Department of Health should be urged to consider that *any life-transforming decisions (or 'choices') by a known vulnerable adult – such as discontinuing a support service – should result in assessments of a person's decision-making capacity* (Flynn, 2007, 7.26).

Comment

The interface between capacity issues and safeguarding issues will be elucidated further in Chapter 6, and some of the lessons and implications of serious case reviews such as those referred to here will be further considered in Chapter 8.

The general point, though, in relation to capacity, is worth restating: that is, if there are any clues that there may be a lack of capacity in relation to a decision, a formal assessment of capacity should be considered. If, after taking steps to help the person make an autonomous decision, it is clear that capacity is lacking, then the difficulty of balancing the competing priorities of supporting independence and preventing harm to the vulnerable needs to filter through the lens of the best interests decision-making process (see Chapter 5).

Activity 4.1

You are the social worker for an older woman, Esther, who has been persuaded to go into respite care, after being discovered in an extreme state of neglect and unhygienic circumstances in her own home. Esther has lived alone for many years as a recluse but has always kept dogs. Social services were alerted when the RSPCA were called to the property and discovered 40 dead dogs there as well as piles of dog and human excrement. It is suspected that Esther has dementia, but she has no diagnosis and has not been known to services. Esther has not visited her GP in many years; she does have daughters but has no contact with them.

A consultant psychiatrist visits Esther at the care home after she has been there a week and carries out a capacity assessment with regard to her ability to make the decision to return home, as she insists she wants. The conclusion is that Esther has capacity and is making an unwise decision.

What would you do? – you may wish to choose more than one option from the following.

A. Accept this assessment and respect Esther's right to make an unwise decision, but worry about the consequences of her living in such conditions and how you are going to support her.
B. Carry out your own capacity assessment and try to gather more information from other sources.
C. Ask for a second opinion and, if necessary, consider approaching the Court of Protection.

Comment

Hopefully, you have selected option B, followed by option C. As stressed in the previous section, any suggestion of vulnerability should mean that you are alert to the need to carry out your own capacity assessment. This assessment should involve you attempting to empower Esther to make her own decision and remembering her right to make an unwise decision. While this may or may not result in the same outcome as that reached by the consultant psychiatrist, you will still have the option of getting a second opinion or approaching the court for a ruling. This scenario is based on a real case, where the social worker was able to track down a vet who had known 'Esther' well and who helpfully provided evidence that previously she would not have allowed herself or her animals to live in such conditions.

Assessing capacity: the two-stage test

While promoting the concept of capacity, the Act does not give this an actual definition, but does define incapacity in section 2. This is known as part 1 of the two-stage test:

> For the purposes of this Act, a person lacks capacity in relation to a matter if at the material time he is unable to make a decision for himself in relation to the matter because of an impairment of or disturbance in the functioning of the mind or brain.

As cited earlier, there can be confusion and reluctance around identifying *an impairment of or disturbance in the functioning of the mind or brain*. It is worth noting that this definition does not require the assessor to identify a formal diagnosis for the individual being assessed and some would argue could possibly encompass people in states of shock or under extreme duress.

Such an approach to satisfying what is often known as the 'diagnostic test' would be legally questionable unless there was also evidence of some other condition such as mental health problems, learning disability or dementia, brain injuries or a physical condition which was affecting a person's thought processes. However, this can be an area of challenge between the legislation and applying it in practice. The principles are clear that a person's decision-making abilities should be maximised in the best possible setting but this is assessing capacity in an ideal situation. If a vulnerable adult is being exploited or abused, his or her decision-making abilities may be very different if given time and distance away from the scene of abuse, as opposed to where he or she is under duress. When, how and where you carry out capacity assessments may produce different outcomes. You will need to be mindful of such factors and the need to revisit capacity assessments after any change in circumstances.

Part 1 of the assessment clearly indicates that capacity needs to be treated as time- and decision-specific. When working with individuals with complex needs, it is sometimes difficult to work out which decision or decisions you need to be assessing for. For example, if working with Carl (see pages 6–7), the capacity assessment would be for his decision to leave home and live independently, but this apparently simple question might involve a substratum of questions, including his capacity to understand and manage his finances and his capacity to understand his support needs independent of his home environment. These questions could be asked of any young person leaving home and section 2(3) makes clear that we should not be subjecting people to discrimination:

> A lack of capacity cannot be established merely by reference to a person's age or appearance, or a condition of his, or an aspect of his behaviour, which might lead others to make unjustified assumptions about his capacity.

Equally, Carl's potential vulnerability and his mother's views may influence our decision to carry out an assessment of capacity or not. As the social worker in this case, you may be keen to enhance Carl's capacity by helping him gain the skills he needs to live independently but there will be always be scope for interpreting information differently:

> In our experience the assessment of capacity varies significantly between assessors, whilst it may be inevitable that different people hold different views on best interests, it is more worrying that whether someone is judged to lack capacity may be strongly influenced by who carries out the assessment.

(Victoria Butler-Cole, 39 *Essex Street Newsletter*, May 2014)

While this subjectivity in assessments can be a pitfall, there is a clear process by which capacity should be assessed. If you are satisfied that you have established 'an impairment of or disturbance in the functioning of the mind or brain' as in section 2, you then proceed to section 3 (part 2 of a two-stage test). A person is said to lack capacity for a specific decision if he/she is unable:

- to understand the information relevant to the decision or
- to retain the information relevant to the decision or
- to use or weigh the information as part of the process of making the decision or
- to communicate the decision by any means.

Consider the following in relation to assessing capacity with Rosemary.

Case Study 4.3

How will you assess Rosemary's capacity to decide where she should go on discharge from hospital?

How will you find out if Rosemary might regain capacity or has made her wishes known prior to developing a dementia?

What other decisions may you need to assess Rosemary's capacity for?

Comment

When completing a capacity assessment with Rosemary or Carl, you will need to make a clear record of how you attempted to enable them to make their own decisions as well as documenting any two-stage tests you carry out. It may be that you will need to allocate several sessions of work with individuals before you feel able to do a formal capacity assessment. Equally, some practitioners find it useful to do an initial capacity assessment with an individual and then return to do it again at a later date. As a social worker, you may be thinking about the risks and unknown safeguarding issues inherent in Rosemary returning to live at home, but going through the process of the two-stage test should help you focus on the actual information available and Rosemary's ability to understand this, thus reducing the risk of a subjective judgement.

The House of Lords Committee (2014) has identified that the quality of capacity assessments is frequently poor and that some social workers did not feel equipped to undertake capacity assessments, and that a lack of confidence was to be found more widely among professionals working in hospitals and care homes *(p37). Such a finding supports the need to give time and consideration to any capacity assessments you undertake and to document the process alongside any standard paperwork used in organisations for the two-stage test.*

Research Summary 4.2

Assessing capacity

Given the complexity and challenges of assessing capacity, a number of researchers have sought to establish whether standardised assessment tools can be helpful and reliable aids to assessment.

The MacCAT-T (MacArthur Competence Assessment Tool for Treatment) is a tool often used in psychiatry to assess capacity to make treatment decisions.

The MMSE (mini mental state examination) is widely used to measure cognitive impairment. While a person with a low score on this measure can still make capable decisions

(Continued)

(Continued)

(Hotopf, 2013) it has been shown that there is a good positive correlation between the MMSE and mental capacity assessments, and it has been suggested that the MMSE can be useful particularly in cases of disputed capacity assessments (Gregory et al., 2007). The MMSE is a well-validated tool which takes about ten minutes to complete.

A systematic review by Okai et al. (2007) found that *studies are consistent in showing the reliability of mental capacity assessments, and these measurements are correlated with indicators of clinical severity but not with demographic differences.* They found that, particularly where standardised measures such as the MacCAT-T were used, several raters were able to decide on whether capacity was present or absent with a high level of agreement. They go on to suggest that this indicates that mental capacity can be reliably measured.

Comment

The kinds of assessment tools referred to above may often be thought of as the preserve of psychiatrists and of little relevance to social workers. What the research illustrates, though, is that information from standardised assessment tools such as these can be used to assist any practitioner in more reliably arriving at judgement about mental capacity. Given the difficulties and challenges of such assessment any such assistance should be welcomed.

Activity 4.2

Below we have listed the potential capacity assessments that need to be carried out with Rosemary. First, identify which of these you feel you should undertake as a social worker, which you will wish to do jointly with the MDT and which you think should be done by nursing staff. (There is very helpful guidance in Chapter 4 of the *Code of Practice* (see Further Reading) about who should carry out assessments.) Second, consider which assessments you need to do now and which could wait. Reflect on what questions you might ask Rosemary and how you would reassure and respect her during this process:

A. Does R have capacity to consent to care and treatment on the ward?
B. Does R have capacity to decide to leave the ward?
C. Does R have capacity to decide where she should live on discharge?
D. Does R have capacity to decide whether to have contact with Hilary, her daughter from whom she has been estranged?
E. Does R have capacity to give you permission to consult with Hilary and her nephew and carer Mark?

Comment

It may be a challenge for you or others to complete points D and E, and these assessments may not be immediately obvious when you have been tasked with assessing Rosemary for a 24-hour placement, but if Rosemary is lacking capacity, there is a duty to make decisions on her behalf in her best interests in every area that she lacks capacity for. How you approach contact with Mark and/or Hilary will depend on whether you are consulting them in Rosemary's best interests or whether she has given you permission to talk with them.

If Rosemary has previously made her wishes known regarding care and treatment options, you may need to speak to Hilary and/or Mark about this and whether they are aware of any advance statements or advance decisions she may have made. It is possible to check with the Office of the Public Guardian, whether there is an LPA registered or a deputy appointed for health and welfare decisions. Depending on the outcome of your research, you may find that there are obstacles to you or others making certain decisions on Rosemary's behalf in her best interests. (Please see Chapters 7, 8 and 9 of the Mental Capacity Act Code of Practice [*see Further Reading*] *for more information.)*

Joint working and links to other legislation

As suggested in the above exercise, there will be areas where as a social worker you may find that you wish to carry out a capacity assessment in conjunction with another profession. The *Code of Practice* (2007) is clear that the practitioner responsible for assessing capacity is *usually … the person who is directly concerned with the individual at the time the decision needs to be made* (section 4.38). This means that if a surgeon is proposing an operation, he or she is responsible for assessing the person's capacity to consent to this treatment, but the guidance does go on to suggest *In settings such as hospital, this can involve the multi disciplinary team* (section 4.40).

In practice, there is sometimes confusion and reluctance from healthcare professionals about who should be conducting capacity assessments. In particular, where a service user has known mental health problems or a learning disability but requires a physical intervention or treatment, those performing the intervention will often request that a mental health professional is responsible for the capacity assessment, stating they do not have sufficient knowledge or expertise in this area to judge how such disabilities may affect capacity. The mental health professional then often rightly argues back that the healthcare practitioner has responsibility for the capacity assessment for the physical intervention as they are best placed to understand the nature of the treatment and its possible outcomes, and thus have the relevant information with which to carry out part 2 of the two-stage test. These arguments can, if not resolved quickly, at best delay treatment for a vulnerable adult and at worst result in an individual not receiving the necessary treatment at all.

Proactive joint working should resolve these disputes. Either a professional in mental health or learning disability could confirm in writing that part 1 of the two-stage test was met, or time could be made by both practitioners to do the capacity assessment together.

The House of Lords Committee (2014) has identified the need for more training for healthcare professionals, especially GPs, to improve their awareness of their responsibilities under the Act (recommendation 7) and hopefully this may reduce such incidences where capacity is either overlooked or becomes an obstacle to the person receiving the care and treatment needed.

As a social worker, you have a role in advocating for best practice in such circumstances. Equally, you will need to think about the capacity assessments you are primarily responsible for and where input from a different discipline will help with this task. If you are newly qualified and feel you do not have sufficient experience or knowledge of a certain client group, involving or consulting others who do may be valuable.

The Mental Capacity Act does not sit in isolation and where there are complex decisions to be made about different forms of care and treatment for a vulnerable adult, it will sometimes be necessary to have discussions around whether the Mental Health Act should be used either as an alternative to the MCA, or in conjunction with it. The interaction between the two pieces of legislation is complex and we will explore this further in Chapter 6.

It is worth remembering that an individual who is deemed to have capacity to refuse treatments for a mental disorder may still be subject to the provisions of the Mental Health Act and thus possibly could be detained for treatment under this law. Young people under the age of 16 do not fall within the scope of the MCA, but a child can be assessed and treated under the Mental Health Act. Any decisions around care and treatment for those under 16 which fall outside the statutory provisions of the Mental Health Act should be made in accordance with child care legislation.

Top tips – how to do a capacity assessment

- Consider carefully which decision or decisions need to be made.
- Involve, as far as possible, those who have expert knowledge and experience in relation to the individual and the issues and impairments which may limit capacity (e.g. specialists in brain injury, Down's syndrome, etc.).
- Think about the best time to complete the assessment.
- Think about the most suitable environment to complete the assessment.
- Use different methods of communication where necessary or find someone who can.
- Take time to provide clear information to the person about the decision to be made and consider carefully their responses.
- Do not confuse your capacity assessment with your risk assessment.

Mental capacity and advocacy

The Independent Mental Capacity Advocate service provides a safeguard and a greater voice for thousands of people in decisions that are fundamentally important.

(House of Lords, 2014)

The role of the IMCA, which was enshrined as a very important part of the Mental Capacity Act, has been widely welcomed as providing a very valuable and valued voice for the vulnerable.

The IMCA provides a voice for a vulnerable person at a time when major decisions in their life need to be taken, and they do not have the voice of family or friends to represent them. In certain situations individuals have a statutory right, under the MCA, to the services of an independent advocate to assist them. At the moment these include decisions about serious medical treatment (under section 37 of the Act) and decisions about change of accommodation when a hospital stay or a move to a care home is involved (under sections 38 and 39). An IMCA must also be involved when applications for authorisation of a deprivation of liberty are made and the person has no other representative.

There is also a discretionary power to provide independent advocacy in other situations, such as in relation to care reviews or adult protection proceedings.

There is ample evidence that referrals to advocacy services have been more routine, and that the system is working better in social care than in healthcare where there have been many decisions relating to serious medical treatment which have not included the representations of an advocate (House of Lords, 2014). This is partly due to a lack of clarity over what constitutes serious medical treatment, but also to lack of awareness and training among health staff of their duties in relation to this.

However, there is no room for complacency in social care. The Neary case in relation to deprivation of liberty (see Chapter 6) and other cases in which social workers have made formal complaints against advocates who questioned their decisions and told them to 'back off' highlight the need for a clear understanding of the role of advocates and an acceptance that their role can be to challenge your decisions in certain cases.

Some have argued that there are inherent conflicts of interest that arise because of the way that independent advocacy services are set up and commissioned. For example, some suggest that, because the advocacy service is commissioned and paid for by the local authority, the advocates who are employed may be reluctant to challenge decisions of local authorities or the social workers employed by them. Where they do challenge decisions, they may be met with responses such as those described above, which may lead them to be more fearful of providing a truly independent voice in the future.

It has now been recommended that a form of self-referral be set up in order that the lengthy delays which have been developing and the conflicts of interest which have been seen can both be avoided.

IMCAs – key points

- An IMCA must be provided to assist a person who has been assessed as lacking capacity to make decisions regarding serious medical treatment or accommodation in a hospital or care home when the person has no one to speak on their behalf.

- When an application has been made under the Deprivation of Liberty Safeguards (DOLS) an IMCA must be appointed where there is not an appropriate person to consult about the proposed course of action.

- It is good practice and now recommended that an IMCA is appointed in all DOLS cases.

- Local authorities have powers but not a duty to appoint an IMCA in care reviews or adult protection investigations.

- A local authority or health body must commission independent advocacy services and must have referral procedures in place.

- An IMCA has the right to consult you if you are a paid worker involved in the care of the person that they represent. They also have the right to look at care records.

- The IMCA should meet the person who lacks capacity, in private, in order to obtain an independent view of the situation and to ascertain as far as possible the person's wishes and feelings.

- It is important to remember that the role of the advocate is to represent the wishes and feelings of the person concerned. It is not to be an independent judge of what is in the person's best interests.

Becoming a social worker

We have made frequent references to the House of Lords report of 2014 which provided some fairly trenchant post-legislative scrutiny of the Mental Capacity Act. In its official response to that report, the government suggested the following.

> The … ambition for the future is that all qualified social workers will have received training in the Mental Capacity Act. A social worker must be able to conduct best interests decisions to fulfil their professional obligations as is the same for all qualified health and social care professionals.

(HM Government, 2014, p12)

This highlights the fact that the Mental Capacity Act is becoming more central to social work practice with adults and also reminds practitioners that a sound understanding of the Act is imperative for safe, effective and up-to-date practice. These points are further emphasised by the new *Knowledge and Skills Statement* (KSS) *for Social Workers in Adult Services* for Adult Social Work produced by the Department of Health in 2015. In relation to the MCA it stipulates the following:

> Social workers must have a thorough knowledge and understanding of the Mental Capacity Act (MCA) and Code of Practice and be able to apply these in practice.
>
> (Department of Health, 2015, section 5)

The statement goes on to make clear the levels of knowledge and skills required as you complete your ASYE:

> By the end of the Assessed and Supported Year in Employment social workers working in an adult setting … [must] be able to understand and work within the legal frameworks relevant to adult settings, in particular, the Mental Capacity Act, Mental Health Act and the Care Act, and fully operate within the organisational context, policies and procedures. They will be able to confidently undertake mental capacity assessments in routine situations; to identify and work proactively and in partnership around safeguarding issues and have demonstrated the ability to work effectively in more complex situations.
>
> (Department of Health, 2015, section 11)

Chapter Summary

In this chapter, we have noted the context which led to the Mental Capacity Act and have tried to elucidate how the five principles and the two-stage test of capacity can be interpreted and implemented in practice. We have also highlighted the importance of independent advocacy in relation to the whole process and the difference which sound advocacy can make. There are other important aspects of the Act which practitioners need to be aware of, including the role of the Court of Protection, Lasting Powers of Attorney and other mechanisms of decision making. You will find more information on these matters in Chapters 3, 5 and 6. It is clear that after a number of years on the statute book knowledge of the Act is increasing but understanding of how to implement it remains less widespread. This partly reflects the genuine complexity and sensitive and sophisticated decision making which is required in many cases. We hope that the guidance in this chapter and others will assist in this difficult process.

Further Reading

The Social Care Institute for Excellence (SCIE) website has a range of useful resources, including e-learning packages, which can assist in understanding how to implement the MCA. See www.scie.org.uk/topic/keyissues/mentalcapacity.

There are some useful audit tools which can help you to check that you are following the necessary steps and making appropriate decisions in relation to the MCA.

The Health and Social Care Advisory Service provides audit tools both for assessing individual practice with a single service user and also for assessing the practice of a ward or care home. See http://mca-audit-tool.hascas.org/.

In a similar vein, the Mental Health Foundation also offers audit tools and advice together with a number of illustrative case studies – see www.amcat.org.uk.

An in-depth review of the Mental Capacity Act by the House of Lords heard evidence from a range of expert witnesses. Its report contains many useful recommendations. See House of Lords Select Committee on the Mental Capacity Act 2005, Report of session 2013–2014. The *Code of Practice*, issued after the passing of the Mental Capacity Act, remains a very good source of advice and guidance. This can be easily accessed from the Ministry of Justice website – see www.justice.gov.uk/downloads/protecting-the-vulnerable/mca/mca-code-practice-0509.pdf.

Chapter 5

Best interests

Meeting professional standards

This chapter will help you to develop the following selected capabilities, to the appropriate level, from the social work Professional Capabilities Framework.

Diversity

- Recognise oppression and discrimination by individuals or organisations and implement appropriate strategies to challenge.

Rights, justice and economic well-being

- Address oppression and discrimination, applying the law to protect and advance people's rights, recognising how legislation can constrain or advance these rights.
- Apply in practice principles of human, civil rights and equalities legislation, and manage competing rights, differing needs and perspectives.

Knowledge

- Demonstrate knowledge and application of appropriate legal and policy frameworks and guidance that inform and mandate social work practice.
- Apply legal reasoning, using professional legal expertise and advice appropriately, recognising where scope for professional judgement exists.
- Understand forms of harm and their impact on people, and the implications for practice, drawing on concepts of strength, resilience, vulnerability, risk and resistance, and apply to practice.

Intervention and skills

- Demonstrate clear communication of evidence-based professional reasoning, judgements and decisions, to professional and non-professional audiences.

Introduction

> Principle 4: *An act done, or decision made, under the Act for or on behalf of a person who lacks capacity must be done, or made, in best interests.*

In this chapter we explore this fundamental principle of the MCA and how it can be worked through in practice. We hope to identify the strengths and pitfalls of best interests decision making in relation to social work practice with vulnerable adults through discussion and by using the two main case studies running through this book. We will highlight common areas of misconception and the challenges involved in applying this principle correctly within a landscape of ever-decreasing resources.

Definition and misconceptions

The Mental Capacity Act 2005 gives us a clear process for identifying best interests when making decisions for those who have been assessed as lacking capacity in relation to specific decisions at a certain point in time. You will find this in section 4 and for ease of reference we have transcribed this in full below.

(1) In determining for the purposes of this Act what is in a person's best interests, the person making the determination must not make it merely on the basis of:

    (a) the person's age or appearance, or

    (b) a condition of his, or an aspect of his behaviour, which might lead others to make unjustified assumptions about what might be in his best interests.

(2) The person making the determination must consider all relevant circumstances and, in particular, take the following steps.

(3) He must consider:

    (a) whether it is likely that the person will at some time have capacity in relation to the matter in question, and

    (b) if it appears likely that he will, when that is likely to be.

(4) He must, so far as reasonably practicable, permit and encourage the person to participate, or improve his ability to participate, as fully as possible in any act done for him and any decision affecting him.

(5) Where the determination relates to life-sustaining treatment he must not, in considering whether the treatment is in the best interests of the person concerned, be motivated by a desire to bring about his death.

(6) He must consider, so far as is reasonably ascertainable:

    (a) the person's past and present wishes and feelings (and, in particular, any relevant written statement made by him when he had capacity),

(b)   the beliefs and values that would be likely to influence his decision if he had capacity, and

(c)   the other factors that he would be likely to consider if he were able to so.

(7)   He must take into account, if it is practicable and appropriate to consult them, the views of:

(a)   anyone named by the person as someone to be consulted on the matter in question or on matters of that kind,

(b)   anyone engaged in caring for the person or interested in his welfare,

(c)   any donee of a Lasting Power of Attorney granted by the person, and

(d)   any deputy appointed for the person by the court, as to what would be in the person's best interests and, in particular, as to matters mentioned in subsection (6).

(8)   The duties imposed by subsections (1) to (7) also apply in relation to the exercise of any powers which:

(a)   are exercisable under a Lasting Power of Attorney, or

(b)   are exercisable by a person under this Act where he reasonably believes that another person lacks capacity.

(9)   In the case of an act done, or a decision made, by a person other than the court, there is sufficient compliance with this section if (having complied with the requirements of subsections (1) to (7)) he reasonably believes that what he does or decides is in the best interests of the person concerned.

(10)   'Life-sustaining treatment' means treatment which in the view of a person providing health care for the person concerned is necessary to sustain life.

(11)   'Relevant circumstances' are those:

(a)   of which the person making the determination is aware, and

(b)   which it would be reasonable to regard as relevant.

We will look at how to apply this process and the individual requirements of the checklist later, but it is worth noting at this point that there is no clear definition of 'best interests' in the legislation. The requirement for the decision maker to consider 'all relevant circumstances' might be common sense, but is also rather vague. The House of Lords Committee report (2014) makes frequent reference to the fact that the fundamental principles of the Mental Capacity Act have been misunderstood or misapplied:

> *However, all too often 'best interests' is interpreted in a medical/paternalistic sense which is wholly at odds with that set out in the Act. Dr Claud Reynard put it more strongly: 'the term best interests is probably the most abused and misunderstood phrase in health and social care'.*

(p45)

It is fair to ask why this has happened over the last seven years that the law has been in force. One supposition is that practitioners get as far as completing the two-stage test for capacity and then feel that this somehow gives them permission to act in a paternalistic way or, more bluntly, that they now have ownership of that vulnerable person to make decisions as they see best. Such a position may sound like anathema to you as a trainee or newly qualified social worker, but imagine having a caseload of 40 adults, where the majority may lack capacity for certain decisions, and the ensuing pressure to resolve and close cases as soon as possible. The temptation to identify a 24-hour placement for Rosemary (see pages 4–6) as soon as possible in the name of 'best interests' will be strong. It may appear time efficient and sensible to quickly assess Rosemary's capacity in relation to the decision to move into 24-hour care, concludes she lacks this and make the decision for her, with token regard for her wishes and feelings.

Institutional settings can be equally at risk of misappropriating the term 'best interests', sometimes citing this as a cover for their own funding or staffing issues. For example, 'an older person with dementia living in a 24-hour placement is not allowed out of that setting because he/she would come to harm' actually translates as 'there is insufficient staff or flexibility within the rota to support the person to go out with a member of staff'. While case law suggests that 'best interests' should be established within available resources, there remains the ethical question of how far it is acceptable to move away from the intentions of the legislation in the name of scant resource.

The House of Lords Committee report (2014) identifies that the concept of best interests is particularly misunderstood in medical settings, citing feedback from the charity, Headway:

> *Staff defined a 'best interests' decision as a 'clinical decision' – and just saw it as a matter of clinical judgement. From the moment of my sister's accident it was if she belonged to them, they were not interested in what we knew about her or her wishes.*

(p46)

Such descriptions are sadly not uncommon, especially where family members challenge or raise questions about a proposed plan of care or treatment. There is a risk where any challenge of a professional view of best interests by family or friends can escalate into disharmony and a dispute. Sometimes such disputes can lead to family or carers being labelled as a safeguarding risk to the vulnerable person. This is not to say that there may be genuine safeguarding concerns when a family member objects to a proposed plan of care and treatment in a vulnerable person's best interests, but as a social worker you need to be alert to the risk described above and whether there are genuine safeguarding issues or whether there is a professional or bureaucratic culture dictating without giving adequate regard to the wishes and feelings of the vulnerable person or those who care for them. We will explore how you might be able to work through such situations at best interests meetings later in the chapter.

One of the most common misconceptions in applying the best interests principle has been around the need to prevent a vulnerable person coming to harm and the weight this consideration is understandably afforded over the other legal requirements of section 4, such as considering the wishes and feelings of the person or the views of other people. It is worth stressing that nowhere in the checklist above does it mention the necessity to prevent a person coming to harm, although this would be included in the consideration of 'all relevant factors'. There is no guidance within the legislation as to the weight that decision makers should give to different elements of the checklist when applying it in order to reach a best interests decision and this can make it a challenging process:

> This section sets out a checklist of factors which must be considered before the decision is made, or the act is carried out. In effect, the checklist establishes the course of action that should be followed in order to reach a determination whether a decision is in the person's best interests, a term which is not defined in the Act. In other words, it deals with the process of acquiring evidence, rather than specifying the criteria of best interests. A considerable latitude is therefore granted to the decision-maker when reaching a reasonable belief as to where P's best interests lie.

(Jones, 2012, p31)

As indicated above, there is a clear responsibility on you as a decision maker within the field of social work, to gather evidence and information to inform the decisions you make on behalf of people who lack capacity, but how you prioritise the different, sometimes competing, factors is left open to your discretion. The statutory checklist above points out what information you should consider and how you should not make discriminatory assumptions. This is the place to start.

Checklists

Many organisations and providers have developed their own summaries of the two-stage capacity assessment (see Chapter 4) and the best interests checklist so that their staff can use these when making best interests decisions and record this as their protection against liability:

> It is also good practice for healthcare and social care staff to record at the end of the process why they think a specific decision is in a person's best interests. This is particularly important if healthcare and social care staff go against the views of somebody who has been consulted while working out the person's best interests.

(MCA *Code of Practice*, Department of Health, 2007, 5.52)

While such documents do require staff to focus on the main elements of the statutory checklist in section 4, often they are designed in a tick-box format which, if used in a perfunctory manner, will lead to token regard to and consideration of to the empowering ethos of the legislation and the requirement to be person-centred when making decisions. As a trainee or newly qualified social worker, you will be expected to follow your employer's own policy and procedure documents for best interests decision making, but there is nothing to stop you adding further information on how you have considered the wishes, feelings, values and beliefs of the person concerned as opposed to simply ticking a box to say that you have.

As explained in Chapter 4, there will be different types of decision to be considered and made for vulnerable adults and the best interests process must be followed in relation to each specific decision that someone has been assessed as lacking capacity for. This will seem daunting to carers or nurses working in very busy environments and may result in the tick-box approach described above. The type of best interests decisions you will need to make as a social worker will not necessarily be as numerous as those required of a team of care staff in a 24-hour placement (for example, best interests decisions about medical treatment, personal care, ability to leave the environment unescorted), but your role is more likely to relate to major decisions in a person's life. For example, should Rosemary (see pages 4–6) be placed in 24-hour care or should she return home?

Where there are such major decisions, it is advisable to hold a best interests meeting in order to ensure that all involved are given the opportunity to contribute to the discussions around best interests. Such practice is advised by the MCA *Code of Practice* where there are disputes (see Chapter 5, para 5.68), but even where there are no disputes, a best interests meeting can be a way of carefully considering and implementing the section 4 checklist.

Activity 5.1

You are asked to assess a young woman (Maisie) with autism and moderate learning disabilities for an adult placement. Maisie lives at home with her parents but has recently been displaying an increase in challenging behaviours, resulting in her parents feeling unable to cope any longer. All involved are in agreement that Maisie lacks the capacity to make this decision for herself and that the way forward is for Maisie to move into a placement in her best interests. How would you proceed?

1. Assume that Maisie lacks capacity because her family and other professionals state this is the case and go ahead with identifying a placement and funding as quickly as possible due to the stress Maisie's parents are experiencing. Then facilitate the move in Maisie's best interests without holding a formal meeting.

or

2. Meet Maisie and her family and start the process of a capacity assessment, trying to support her first to make her own decision. You establish that Maisie does lack capacity to make this decision but in the process find out some of Maisie's likes and dislikes around activities and her environment. Then identify a choice of placements and hold a formal best interests meeting, with Maisie and her parents involved, to make the decision about the move and which placement.

Comment

Comment

Hopefully, you have selected option 2 as you have a duty under the law to make the capacity assessment for the decision to move into a placement and this process (see Chapter 4) should enable you to become familiar with Maisie, her needs, and her likes and dislikes. A best interests meeting will enable you to think about all aspects of the decision being made, not just the need to keep Maisie and her parents safe. In crisis situations, where there are immediate risks which cannot be reduced by extra support in the home, it would not be inconceivable to go with option 1, but you would need to follow up afterwards with the steps described in 2.

Using the statutory checklist

As cited above, there is frequently a temptation to skip through the requirements of section 4 in order to justify a decision that may have already been made in the minds of professionals or family members. The best interests principle, however, dictates that all involved should take a person-centred approach and not make a decision on behalf of a vulnerable person, until their individual circumstances have been considered and appraised:

> Each human being is unique and, thus, best interests decisions are unique to that human being. In almost every case, it should be enough to test the facts of the case against the relevant statutory provisions in order to ascertain the unique solution to that particular case.

(Jones, 2012, p33)

While many practitioners would agree with this statement, the challenge inherent in this approach is whether you, as a social worker, have access to the resources that would allow you to create the 'unique solution' for each person. We will try to suggest a few answers to this conundrum at the end of the chapter.

Whether you are holding a best interests meeting or not, the first requirement of section 4 echoes that in section 2, namely to be non-discriminatory in how you make decisions. In Carl's scenario (see pages 6–7), you may have already established that he has the capacity to make the decision to live independently, but if you found that he did not, the first part of the checklist dictates that you and others do not make 'unjustified assumptions' because of his age, condition or behaviour. This should be second nature to you as a social worker, but when discussing Carl's case with others, such as medical staff, you may have to challenge any such discrimination.

The next step is to 'consider all relevant circumstances', which often will involve the consideration of risk, need and available resources. Subsection 11 of section 4 does give a definition of relevant circumstances as (a) 'of which the person making the determination is aware' and (b) 'which it would be reasonable to regard as relevant'. Brown and Barber (2008) suggest that *This allows for a degree of flexibility so that one would not have to make exhaustive enquiries in every set of circumstances* (p30). However, within the consideration of all relevant circumstances is the requirement to focus on key aspects. We will discuss those most relevant to you as a social worker. Please read the following in conjunction with the transcribed checklist at the beginning of the chapter.

Subsection 3: This step encourages you to revisit your capacity assessment. In Rosemary's scenario, you have assessed her as lacking capacity to make the decision as to where she should go on discharge from hospital, but in any best interests consideration it is vital you think about whether she is likely to regain this capacity and, if so, when. For example, is Rosemary suffering from a urinary tract infection which, if treated, might result in her regaining capacity? For those cases where individuals have suffered head injuries, it may be difficult to ascertain if and when they might regain capacity and consultation and/or joint working with other MDT members or specialists such as neuropsychologists will be key in being able to meet this step fully. If you have reason to suspect that an individual may regain capacity for a particular decision in the near future, then the MCA tells us we should wait rather than make a best interests decision on their behalf.

Subsection 4: This step can often be lost within the best interests process, when practitioners decide that it will be too distressing for the individual concerned to be involved in the decision making. However, this step dictates that the person should participate or be empowered to do so as far as 'reasonably practicable'. If working with an individual with limited verbal communication skills, you might want to use communication aids such as PECS. For people suffering from cognitive impairment, you will need to think about how you present information to them and what you can use as memory prompts. For all service users, it is vital to consider the use of an IMCA to support them in expressing their views and wishes (see Chapter 4). Vulnerable individuals should not be excluded from best interests meetings just because they may get upset, but you may wish to think about whether the person stays for the full meeting or whether they attend for an allocated slot to put their views across. If the person is not entitled to an IMCA, because there are family involved who are deemed appropriate to consult, then there is nothing to stop you approaching a general advocate to support the vulnerable person.

Subsection 6: Again, the checklist pushes you back to the individual concerned, their past and present wishes and feelings, beliefs, values and factors that they would consider relevant if they were able to do so. It is worth noting here that you are tasked with trying to find out what an individual might have considered relevant for themselves, when they had capacity. This might involve asking family members, but also involves a degree of conjecture. When asking family members about what a loved one might have wanted or considered relevant to the decision, remember that they might be expressing a personal preference for themselves. This step sounds straightforward, but in the absence of any written statement from the person themselves, it is best not to assume too much. You should, however, consider the following:

- cultural background;

- religious beliefs;

- political convictions; or

- past behaviour or habits (see MCA *Code of Practice*, 5.46).

Subsection 7: This step involves consultation with family, friends and/or anyone with decision-making powers for the individual concerned such as deputies or those who have Lasting Powers of Attorney. In some ways this can be the most challenging step in the checklist, particularly if there are relatives who disagree about the person's best interests. One risk is that carers will speak about their own needs, especially if they have struggled to receive support from statutory services up until the point of the best interests decision being made. It is important to remember that carers will need their own needs assessing separately from the best interests decision-making process in order for the focus to remain on the vulnerable person. Other challenges within this requirement include how widely to consult and how you balance the individual's right to confidentiality when you are consulting, particularly if there are safeguarding concerns around a carer's behaviour. As a social worker, you will need to think carefully about who you are consulting and why. You will also need skills in asking questions without necessarily giving too much information away:

> Decision makers must balance the duty to consult other people with the right to confidentiality of the person who lacks capacity. So if confidential information is to be discussed, they should only seek the views of people who it is appropriate to consult, where their views are relevant to the decision to be made and the particular circumstances.

> (MCA *Code of Practice*, 5.56)

It is evident from the above discussion that there are challenges in how you carry out the steps in the statutory checklist and you will need time and clear communication skills to do this thoroughly. When working under pressure, the temptation to rush through some of these will be great and this is before you have begun to weigh the information you gather and actually make a best interests decision. If you need to challenge a line manager about the time you need to give to the process, it may be worth referring them to the following.

> It's important not to take shortcuts in working out best interests, and a proper and objective assessment must be carried out on every occasion.

> (MCA *Code of Practice*, 5.13)

Whatever the challenges, the ethos of the legislation is for empowerment and person-centred assessments. This framework will give you opportunity to challenge the political landscape in which you work with its clear focus on the individual, not on service provision or local policy.

Activity 5.2

Consider the above in relation to Rosemary; in particular, focus on the following questions:

(a) You decide to organise a best interests meeting on the ward. Who should you invite?
(b) What decision do you hope to make at the meeting?
(c) How will you facilitate everyone making their contributions?
(d) How will you ensure Rosemary is involved and able to express her views?
(e) How will a best interests decision be reached?

Comment

Hopefully, you will be able to begin to answer some of these questions for yourself from your reading so far, in particular those aspects that relate to the statutory checklist. In the next section we hope to help you answer these questions more fully by discussing ways of weighing information and reaching a best interests decision and by offering some guidance around best interests meetings. In Rosemary's scenario there are the additional complications of dispute between the relatives and suspected safeguarding concerns. While this scenario is, of course, fictitious, it is worth saying that such cases are not uncommon and it is important not to get too lost in these complexities, but remain person-centred in your role with Rosemary.

Best interests meetings

When it comes to organising such meetings, it is sometimes difficult to decide who should be invited. This will depend on what decision or decisions you hope to make. Think about Rosemary's scenario and consider whether there is just one decision or maybe several that need to be made. Can you encompass two decisions into one meeting or will you need separate meetings? If you are focused on the question as to whether Rosemary needs to go into a 24-hour placement, then who is going to be the 'decision maker'? The answer should be you as the social worker, but where there are additional safeguarding concerns you may need to consider whether a member of the safeguarding team should take the role of decision maker for decisions about the need to protect Rosemary from her relatives. Ideally, you should retain this role but listen to any information or advice the safeguarding team have to offer as part of consultations under subsection 7.

Where there are safeguarding concerns about carers or family members, they should not be automatically excluded from best interests meetings, but you will need to reflect on how they can contribute without having access to information which could allow further harm to a vulnerable adult. If family are opposed to or challenging the view of professionals, then a best interests meeting can be a good forum for everyone to air their views in a structured way.

As a newly qualified social worker, your job will be made easier by ensuring you have an experienced chair for the meeting. All best interests meetings should have a chairperson to ensure all present are able to contribute and to follow the necessary steps of the checklist. The chairperson ideally should be not involved in the person's case and thus be able to bring a degree of neutrality and independence to a meeting, especially where there are disputes. Where there are arguments between family members over the best interests of a vulnerable adult, the chairperson may need mediation skills and an ability to keep order.

Activity 5.3

Below is a list of people you could invite to a best interests meeting on the ward for Rosemary to make the decision about going home. Try listing these people in order of priority as to who you would want present.

1. The ward manager
2. Nursing staff
3. Mark (nephew and carer but about whom there are suspicions)
4. Rosemary
5. Hilary (Rosemary's daughter, who has been estranged from her)
6. Safeguarding team
7. IMCA
8. An independent chair
9. The manager of an identified care home
10. Occupational therapist
11. Decision maker.

Comment

If you have referred back to the statutory checklist, then hopefully top of your list will be Rosemary, an IMCA, both family members, and a member of nursing staff who is currently involved in Rosemary's treatment and care. In addition to these people you will need the independent chair and you as the decision maker. While it will be very useful for the other people listed to be present, there is no reason why they should not submit their own assessments to the meeting in written form for consideration in the decision making. Equally, if Hilary or Mark declined the invitation and/or were unable to attend, then good practice would suggest that they should be encouraged to give their views to you before the meeting so that they can be considered.

(Continued)

(Continued)

There may be less obvious people to consider inviting to best interests meetings, such as friends or neighbours who have known the person for a long time and who may provide a valuable contribution to the best interests decision. Such people may be particularly important to consult under subsection 7 where there are no family members actively involved in a person's care. Equally, long-term friends can sometimes provide a more objective view of an individual than family members.

What is a best interests decision?

Every day we make many decisions for ourselves; some of these may not be significant and some will be. Some decisions we make will be unwise and some may be very sensible. How we make these decisions will be influenced by a wide range of factors such as how we are feeling at that particular moment, views of peers or family or our own political, cultural or religious beliefs. What is clear is that we do not make decisions in a vacuum. When making a best interests decision, the law is asking us to make a decision for someone else. When this is a serious decision such as where an individual should live, it is important not to underestimate this task.

The ethical issues discussed in Chapter 2 and the other influences on decision making discussed in Chapter 3 are highly pertinent to this consideration of how best to arrive at best interests decisions.

It is worth noting at this point that there is some debate about whether the Mental Capacity Act is compatible with human rights legislation. Article 12 of the Convention on the Rights of Persons with Disabilities states that 'substituted decision making' should be replaced by supported decision making in that *any decision made by a substitute decision maker is based on what is believed to be in the objective 'best interests' of the person concerned, as opposed to being based on the person's own will and preferences* (Court of Protection newsletter, May 2014). Those who drafted the legislation have gone to some lengths in the statutory checklist to ensure that the wishes and views of the person play an important role in the deliberations around best interests, and principle 2 also seems to enshrine the right of the vulnerable or disabled person to make their own decisions with support. As such, it will be interesting to see how this debate progresses.

Before making a best interests decision, it is worth being mindful of the above tensions both within the statutory checklist and within your role as social worker. For example, an older person faced with the prospect of a 24-hour placement may be desperate to return home to their spouse of 50+ years, but their spouse may feel unable to cope with their loved one and feel the placement is necessary in best interests. If as a social worker you had access to resources enabling you to provide a substantial care package to the couple at home, you might be able to resolve such a conflict, but fighting for such resources for one person over another will put you in conflict with your employing organisation's attempt to distribute resources equitably.

There are different ways we make decisions for ourselves and some of these will be affected by our personalities as much as by outside influences or pressures. Impulsivity may be one style; at the opposite end of the spectrum is thorough research into all the options before making a measured choice. Equally, we may make certain decisions out of habit, for example always having cereals for breakfast. When making a best interests decision as a social worker, hopefully you will not do this impulsively or choose a certain care option for somebody out of habit, but being aware of your own decision-making style will improve your ability to try to stay as objective as possible in your role as decision maker for someone else. It is important to remember that a best interests decision is not what we would want for ourselves or loved ones, but is supposed to be an objective choice.

Least restrictive option

When you are considering the information you have gathered by following the steps in the statutory checklist, you have a duty to do this in light of all the principles of the MCA, including principle 5:

> Before the act is done, or the decision made, regard must be had to whether the purpose for which it is needed can be as effectively achieved in a way that is less restrictive of the person's rights and freedom of action.

We will explore this principle in more depth in Chapter 6 in relation to the Deprivation of Liberty Safeguards, but you need to provide evidence as to how any best interests decision you take is the least restrictive option available. When working with adults who are at risk of significant harm, it may be difficult to balance respecting their rights and freedoms against your duty to protect or safeguard them. In Chapter 4 we explored some of these tensions in relation to principle 3, the right to make unwise decisions, but, where an individual has been assessed as lacking capacity for a specific decision, the legislation affords more power to the decision maker to curtail an individual's rights or freedoms. For example, a person with severe autism and learning disabilities may present with challenging behaviours that could cause them or others harm. Physical or chemical interventions may be necessary in their best interests to prevent the individual coming to harm, but such restraints need to be used in the least restrictive way possible. One-to-one staffing for the person might be a less restrictive way to manage these behaviours if the person responds negatively to specified triggers in their environment such as crowds or noise, which a member of care staff could support the person to avoid.

Jones (2012) points out that the best interests principle takes precedence over the least restrictive principle, but that the least restrictive option must always be explored:

> *Someone making a decision or acting on behalf of a mentally incapacitated person must consider whether it is possible to decide or act in a way that would interfere less with the person's rights and freedom of action, or whether there is a need to act at all. Put another way, the intervention should be proportional to the particular circumstances of the case. As only 'regard' must be had to this principle, an option which is not the least restrictive option can still be in the person's best interests.*

(p14)

While the above comment may sound contradictory, we would suggest that such nuances are part of the many layers and aspects that you need to consider and reflect upon in order to make a best interests decision. In some ways it may help to envisage the whole process as an onion, where its layers are both separate and integral to the whole vegetable.

Making the decision

Having explored the principles, process and steps involved in gathering the information you need to make a best interests decision, it is now time to look at how you sort through this to reach a conclusion. This part of the process is often referred to as 'weighing the information', as it requires the decision maker to balance out the sometimes competing requirements described above, for example rights against risk of significant harm, or the wishes and feelings of the person concerned against those of their family.

Option 1: For Rosemary to return home with a care package.

Positives	Risks

Option 2: For Rosemary to move into a 24-hour placement.

Positives	Risks

Figure 5.1 Best interests balance sheet

Comment

A helpful way to do this can be by using what is called a balance sheet (see Figure 5.1). This is a method historically developed by the courts, but as a decision maker within the field of social work, you can use this to good effect without becoming too legalistic in your approach. The idea behind such a tool is that you have two options to decide between – for example, with Rosemary, to go home with a care package or to move into a 24-hour placement – and that you then list all the potential advantages and disadvantages to Rosemary of both options. These advantages and disadvantages should incorporate all aspects of a vulnerable person's well-being, such as emotional and psychological health as well as physical safety. Once you have completed such a list for both options, the idea is that one option will have more advantages to the person than another and this is the best interests decision.

When holding best interests meetings, the chair may wish to use a balance sheet as a visible tool to help all present to contribute to listing advantages and disadvantages for the person. At this point the steps of the checklist should already have been completed, so if there has been any disparity in views of those present, then encouraging everyone present to contribute to the balance sheet may help resolve conflict between family members and professionals. Such a technique can be very useful in preventing disputes escalating, where families feel professionals are dictating to them. While all involved may be part of drawing up a balance sheet, it is important to stress the responsibility for the decision remains with the decision maker.

Decision makers

In Chapter 3 we have explored the historical legal basis for how decisions were made for individuals who were unable to consent to care and treatment before the MCA came into force, and have noted the shift from a more medical approach to a greater weight being given to a person's welfare and well-being. The implementation of the MCA means that health and social care professionals, doctors, care assistants, ambulance staff and a wide array of people can be decision makers under this legislation when a person has been assessed as lacking capacity to consent to care and treatment. Sometimes this process will not involve a formal capacity assessment as detailed in Chapter 4, for example where a care assistant decides what clothes a person should wear in a morning when a person is unable to indicate their own choice in any way. In life-threatening situations, ambulance staff may have to make decisions quickly and assume a lack of capacity. These people will be making decisions in a person's best interests.

As discussed in Chapter 4, the person responsible for an intervention is tasked with carrying out the capacity assessment and it then generally follows that this person becomes the best interests decision maker. As a social worker the most common best interests decisions you will make will be about a person's care needs and/or accommodation.

The MCA, however, also enshrines the concept of other individuals being given decision-making powers in a person's best interests. In particular, there are provisions for family or friends to be appointed as attorneys or deputies under the act in relation to specific areas, either finance or health and welfare. A Lasting Power of Attorney (LPA) can be granted by an individual who has capacity to another to be used at such a time when they are assessed as lacking capacity for specific decisions. At present the LPA has to be registered with the Office of the Public Guardian for it to be valid. Deputies can be appointed by the Court of Protection when an individual already lacks capacity to make certain decisions on their behalf. In addition to these decision makers, the court itself can make best interests decisions, particularly if there is a dispute between family and the statutory services around a vulnerable person's best interests.

NB: If you establish that a family member or friend has an LPA for health and welfare or is acting as a court-appointed deputy for health and welfare decisions for one of your service users, you will need to carry out your capacity assessments, but then the legal authority for decision making will fall to this person and not to you as social worker. Those acting as LPAs or deputies are required to consider and act in a person's best interests in the same way as professionals.

Activity 5.4

Take some time to draw a balance sheet for Rosemary and then complete it as far as you can, assuming that Rosemary wants to return home; that Mark supports this; that Hilary would like to see Rosemary in a placement as she sees Mark as only wanting Rosemary to return home so that he can continue to live there rent free; and that the most substantial care package your employing organisation could offer would be three 20-minute episodes of home care a day. The safeguarding team have some concerns about Mark's reported attitude to leaving Rosemary home alone when he goes out to play golf, but no other concrete information. The occupational therapist on the ward has done a home visit with Rosemary and completed a report indicating that certain aids and adaptations will be necessary if Rosemary is allowed to return home. A bed is available within a local nursing home and Rosemary has been assessed as suitable for this. Remember the person-centred focus of the checklist and see what decision you might make.

Comment

Where you are making best interests decisions as a social worker and do not deem it necessary to hold a meeting, or where all are in agreement with a proposed course of action, it is still a statutory requirement to follow the checklist and to consider the least restrictive option for the person. Equally, it would be good practice for you to draw up a balance sheet for the decision to evidence how you have reached your conclusion.

Balance sheets are not the only way to weigh the information available to you and frequently practitioners will feel that they can reach a best interests decision without these, but we would respectfully suggest that they can prevent the paternalistic and risk-averse approaches identified in the House of Lords Committee report, when information gained by following the checklist correctly is then filtered through this weighing of the pros and cons of one care plan over another. If there are more than two options for a person, then you can add these on to the balance sheet, still breaking each choice up between advantages and disadvantages to your service user.

Risk assessment and best interests decisions

As highlighted at the beginning of this chapter, there is frequently a temptation to look at best interests decisions solely in the light of trying to prevent an adult at risk from coming to harm. It is important not to underestimate risk of harm to an individual when 'considering all relevant factors', but equally this should not be the only criterion for your decision. It would be good practice to complete your risk assessment before going through the processes described above so that this assessment can inform rather than dictate the best interests decision making.

When there are specific safeguarding concerns for an individual, these will, of course, weigh heavily in the decisions that are made, but the wishes and feelings of the person themselves should not be lost. There may be strong emotional bonds between an adult at risk and an individual who is financially exploiting them. A best interests decision or series of decisions should ideally aim to protect an individual assessed as lacking capacity from such harm, but at the same time try to find a way of allowing such a relationship to continue within safe boundaries, if that is what the vulnerable adult wants. Equally, if there are concerns about a carer's ability to continue to deliver care to a vulnerable adult, then it may be possible to look at ways of supporting the person through a carer's assessment rather than automatically concluding that it would not be in the person's best interests to continue to receive care from that person. Best interests decision making should not be conducted in isolation from your other roles and statutory responsibilities as a social worker; nor should it be a substitute for them.

Disputes

As highlighted throughout this chapter, there will be times when there are disputes about a vulnerable adult's best interests. It may be possible for you as a social worker to prevent such disputes escalating by taking time to listen to the different views of those involved and/or by holding best interests meetings to allow a thorough discussion. If, after taking such actions, there remains a dispute over a decision about where a vulnerable adult should live or about the kind of contact they should have with a family member or partner, then there is a duty on local authorities to refer such cases to the Court of Protection. This is primarily because your decision may involve a breach of Article 8 of the Human Rights Act.

> *Our home and family life are central aspects for many of us to our sense of being. Yet social workers frequently have to intervene in family life, for example, moving an older person from her home of 40 years to a safer care home.*

> (Mantell and Scragg, 2009, p40)

As indicated by the above quote, there is an inherent challenge in the social worker's role where it is necessary to intervene and move an adult at risk away from their home or family. Best interests decisions require a sophisticated balancing of rights against responsibilities, where it is necessary to pay regard to the different layers of the legislation. It is interesting to compare this process to that required by child care legislation, where there is a higher legal threshold for removing a child from their family, namely that they must be at risk of 'significant harm', as opposed to such a decision being in their best interests. It is important to remember, though, that while you can make a best interests decision that may infringe on Article 8 if this is proportionate to the risk of harm and others are in agreement with this, any decisions that put you in conflict with family members or where contact between a vulnerable adult and another person is going to be restricted must be passed to the Court of Protection for a legal hearing.

Case Law Summary 5.1

The Court of Protection is frequently approached to make rulings in an individual's best interests. The kinds of cases that are referred to the courts tend to involve the following issues: safeguarding concerns about residence and contact for vulnerable adults; cases where there is a dispute about a person's best interests; and cases concerning medical treatment, often in relation to whether it is in a person's best interests to receive life-sustaining treatment or not. In the first instance the court has to be satisfied that the person concerned lacks capacity to consent to a certain form of care and/or treatment and there are often several independent capacity assessments done before this is ascertained. The reader may find it useful to read the two following cases, which are recent examples of best interests decision making by the courts: *Norfolk CC v PB* [2014] is a case concerning residence and contact and *County Durham and Darlington NHSFT v PP & Ors* [2014], a case about withholding life-sustaining treatment.

Comment

As well as the specific cases mentioned above, it is worth checking on a fairly regular basis for significant updates on case law. You may have access to such updates through your workplace. A good source for such information, which does not require a subscription for access, is: www.localgovernmentlawyer.co.uk.

Care planning at home

So far in this chapter we have focused on best interests decisions that you will have to make as a social worker when considering the need to move a person assessed as lacking capacity from a domestic setting into a placement. There are, of course, many other contexts in which best interests decision making will apply, including medical ones. While decisions about medical treatments will necessarily fall to the relevant medical staff such as nurses, doctors or surgeons, there is a role for hospital-based social workers in discharge planning. In particular there is a role to play when nursing staff are keen to free up a hospital bed and will try to discharge an older adult quickly into a temporary placement without giving full regard to the best interests process and possible alternatives.

If planning a care package for an individual at home or for someone returning home, it will be necessary to follow the principles of the Mental Capacity Act, by assessing a person's capacity if necessary and then planning care in their best interests. If contracting with a home care provider, ideally you should involve them in this process, so that agency staff are aware of the legal framework in which they are operating. This may be important if you think an individual is likely to refuse care, as home carers should be allowed to deliver care with verbal persuasion if that is in the person's best interests. Where an individual is assessed as lacking capacity to manage their finances, this should not preclude any financial contributions they need to make to their care being managed by another person with decision-making powers in this area, such as a financial deputy, LPA for finance or appointee. Equally, direct payments could be offered to a family member to purchase care for their loved one.

Resource issues and new opportunities under the Care Act

Often, providing an individual with a package of care at home will be the least restrictive option for that person, but the resources available to you will frequently constrain this option. For example, it is now virtually impossible in the authors' area to obtain a night sitter for someone. The advent of the Care Act may not improve the amount of resources available but will shift how these are allocated with its statutory emphasis on joint working between health and social care, the recognition of the need for a person-centred approach and the requirement on agencies to try to work in a preventive manner. The Care Act also places greater emphasis on the role and needs of carers. All these aspects of the legislation should in theory allow you to make stronger arguments for the resources needed to make best interests decisions for someone to remain at home. Lynn Romeo (Chief Social Worker for Adults) comments in her annual report (Department of Health, 2014) that the Care Act will provide both opportunities and challenges to social workers and local authorities:

> *This will mean a shift away from a top-down reactive model of care, to one*
> *which centres on wellbeing, prevention and early intervention, helping reduce*
> *crisis and demand for acute services ... Instead of a narrow 'case management,*
> *care planning' approach to support, there will be scope to lead in the sorts*
> *of innovative, strength-based approaches with individuals, families and*
> *communities.*

(p10)

Increasingly, as a social worker, you will have to be creative in how you access support for service users in your local community and/or rely on care provided by families or neighbours. When relying on informal or private carers to help maintain a vulnerable person at home, there is the potential risk of that person being exploited or harmed where there is no oversight of these arrangements.

How far can you go in applying the person-centred ethos of the best interests checklist when the resources available may not be enough to keep a person safe? The answer to this is not straightforward and it will depend on what other sources of support you can identify for a person in the local community, such as that provided by local churches or mosques or voluntary organisations. Equally, it will depend on how far you are prepared to take positive risks in your practice. No package of care at home is ever going to be sufficient to keep a vulnerable person totally safe and, while it is important not to underestimate significant risks facing an older person with dementia who, for example, wanders from their home at night, it is also important to try to look at ways of minimising such risks as opposed to eradicating them completely.

With the rapid expansion of technology in the last 20 years there may be more inventive options available to you to enable a person to remain in their own home, if this is their wish. Many would be appalled at the notion of tagging a person with dementia, but this is an example of a way the risk of someone wandering could be monitored and still allow that person some degree of freedom in a familiar environment. Such an infringement of a person's civil liberties would no doubt involve a deprivation of liberty and this is an area of law and practice we will explore in the next chapter. Lifeline devices and telecare systems are already being used in people's care at home.

The authors would argue that the best interests requirements should also give you the opportunity to be flexible in how you use available resources. As the emphasis on person-centred decision making is so clear, you have the opportunity to argue about how the cost of a standard care package could be used more flexibly in that person's best interests. For example, rather than contract with a home care agency, is there another way the money could be used to allow a person to stay at home? When a person is assessed as having continuing healthcare needs, it can be presumed that these monies will fund a placement as opposed to care at home, but the best interests process should encourage the decision makers to look at funding care at home. It is not necessarily a case of arguing for more resources, as much as practitioners may wish to do this in the name of a civilised society, but of advocating for more flexible ways of allocating resources. However, the challenges remain as the law pushes one way and the resource constraints will frequently push decision makers in the opposite direction. As a social worker, your training should put you in a strong position to understand and recognise these tensions. Best interests decision making will not remove such tensions, but should enable you to work through them.

Becoming a social worker

Throughout this chapter we have focused on the practical aspects of applying the best interests principle within the realm of decisions you may make in your role as social worker. The challenges and nuances of this process will involve you being able to reflect critically on information you gather, listen to different views and take responsibility for decisions you make on behalf of vulnerable adults. It is important that you recognise the tensions inherent in the process and can show that you have acted in accordance with the section 4 checklist. If you wish to avoid misapplying the best interests principle, try not to take shortcuts or use the process to justify outcomes that are already assumed.

Chapter Summary

We hope that this chapter has given you a good understanding of how to make best interests decisions in your role as social worker and the need to consider all aspects of a person's well-being before reaching a conclusion. We have highlighted some of the concerns raised by the House of Lords Committee report around how the best interests principle has been misapplied or misunderstood, and have suggested ways of working through the section 4 checklist to prevent your approach becoming too simplistic or risk-averse. The pressure on available resources will inevitably constrain how you can act in a person's best interests, but this does not mean you bypass the person concerned and make decisions purely consistent with existing service provision.

Further Reading

One of the best and most thorough sources of guidance in relation to best interests decision making remains that published by the British Psychological Society, *Best Interests Guidance on determining the best interests of adults who lack the capacity to make a decision (or decisions) for themselves.* It is widely available to download. Hard copies can be ordered from the society at www.bps.org.uk.

The Mental Health Foundation produces a range of useful resources for care professionals. It has a set of web pages on the subject of best interests decision making (see www.bestinterests.org.uk). A particularly useful feature of this site is the BRIDGET audit tool, which allows you to assess your own practice in relation to standards of good practice.

Chapter 6

Deprivation of Liberty Safeguards (DOLS)

Meeting professional standards

This chapter will help you to develop the following selected capabilities, to the appropriate level, from the social work Professional Capabilities Framework.

Diversity

- Recognise oppression and discrimination by individuals or organisations and implement appropriate strategies to challenge it.
- Identify the impact of the power invested in your role on relationships and your intervention, and be able to adapt your practice accordingly.

Rights, justice and economic well-being

- Address oppression and discrimination applying the law to protect and advance people's rights, recognising how legislation can constrain or advance these rights.
- Apply in practice principles of human, civil rights and equalities legislation, and manage competing rights, differing needs and perspectives.
- Empower service users and carers through recognising their rights and enable access where appropriate to independent advocacy.

Knowledge

- Demonstrate knowledge and application of appropriate legal and policy frameworks and guidance that inform and mandate social work practice.
- Apply legal reasoning, using professional legal expertise and advice appropriately, recognising where scope for professional judgement exists.
- Understand forms of harm and their impact on people, and the implications for practice, drawing on concepts of strength, resilience, vulnerability, risk and resistance, and apply to practice.

- Demonstrate clear communication of evidence-based professional reasoning, judgements and decisions, to professional and non-professional audiences.

Introduction

This chapter will be of most relevance to those who are likely to train as best interests assessors (BIAs). Given that a number of local authorities are arranging for all their adult social workers to train as BIAs, to meet a demand which looks set to remain high for the foreseeable future, this potentially covers a large proportion of the qualified professional workforce.

For those who are unlikely to follow the BIA path, there is still a good deal of information in this chapter which is of relevance to practice. Restrictions on liberty, issues of mental capacity, human rights legislation, lessons from case law for practitioners: all of these have a bearing on the wider scope of adult social care practice.

In this chapter we aim to introduce readers to this complex and fast changing area of the law, including a summary of the Bournewood judgment, the introduction of the Deprivation of Liberty Safeguards (DOLS) framework, and some consideration of how it relates to the safeguarding agenda. In particular we will discuss whether the DOLS are fit for purpose and some of the strengths and weaknesses inherent in the application of the law as it currently stands.

What are the Deprivation of Liberty Safeguards?

The DOLS became law in April 2009 and apply to all people aged 18, residing in a registered care home or hospital, and who are assessed as lacking in consent to their care and treatment in these settings, where they are subject to care and treatment plans that amount to a deprivation of liberty. DOLS were intended to protect vulnerable adults by offering a right of appeal and an independent assessment of their care and treatment.

The problems in knowing where and when these safeguards apply have been centred around a lack of clear definition of what constitutes a deprivation of liberty and this, alongside other factors, has contributed to the wide variation in the use of the safeguards around the country (CQC, 2014). The landmark Cheshire West judgment in March 2014 (see Significant case law section, pages 96–7) may have resolved this by offering an 'acid test' for deprivation, but there still remains significant confusion and panic about this definition. Other problems with the safeguards have been identified as the following: difficulties involved in exercising the right of appeal (obtaining legal aid and advice and speed of access to the Court of Protection); the fact that they only apply to vulnerable individuals in registered care homes and hospitals (not to people in supported living or at home); and a general lack of understanding by care providers of how to use these safeguards.

The House of Lords Committee report (2014) considered the Deprivation of Liberty Safeguards separately from the Mental Capacity Act and concluded:

> *The provisions are poorly drafted, overly complex and bear no relationship to the language and ethos of the Mental Capacity Act. The safeguards are not well understood and are poorly implemented. Evidence suggested that thousands, if not tens of thousands, of individuals are being deprived of their liberty without the protection of the law, and therefore without the safeguards which Parliament intended … The only appropriate recommendation in the face of such criticism is to start again. We therefore recommend a comprehensive review of the Deprivation of Liberty Safeguards with a view to replacing them with provisions that are compatible in style and ethos to the rest of the Mental Capacity Act.*

> (House of Lords, 2014, p93)

This is a clear indictment of the legislation, and initially the government refuted the need to act on this recommendation. There was change of heart within government in September 2014 and there is to be a comprehensive review of the DOLS, by the Law Commission, with a plan to have draft legislation ready for 2017. It may be that a new form of the Deprivation of Liberty Safeguards will be in place by 2018 but, in the meantime, practitioners in health and social care still need to work with the existing law, however faulty or difficult it may be.

The Bournewood judgment

The DOLS were inserted into the Mental Capacity Act by the Mental Health Act 2007 and came into force in April 2009. The legislation was specifically designed to fill a gap in the law as identified by the Bournewood judgment (*HL v UK* [2004]). In Chapter 3 we have provided an historical overview of the legal basis for decision making in health and social care settings, including a discussion of the doctrine of necessity. This doctrine was judged by some to allow the informal treatment of people within a confined setting, but this argument was overturned by the judgment in Bournewood.

HL was a 43-year-old man who had severe autism and lacked capacity to consent to his care and treatment; he had come to live with his foster carers, Mr and Mrs E, in 1994 after spending 32 years living in hospital. HL had no speech and needed significant support and care. In July 1997 the bus driver who drove HL to a day centre once a week took a different route there, which caused HL to display some challenging behaviours on arrival at the day centre. Due to concerns raised by the day centre staff, HL was informally admitted to Bournewood Hospital the same day without any consultation with Mr and Mrs E. HL was then kept in hospital (within a locked ward) and his foster carers were not allowed to discharge him; neither were they allowed contact. Mr and Mrs E were not consulted about these decisions and employed a solicitor. There then followed a series of different legal challenges and judgments in the UK courts about the legality of HL's detention, resulting in the House of Lords ruling in 1998 that HL had not in fact been illegally detained. HL had been allowed to return home to live with his foster carers in December 1997, but Mr and Mrs E were shocked by the condition in which he had returned, and made a video showing him with blackened toenails, scabs on his face and looking undernourished. During his stay in hospital, HL had been put in seclusion and isolation on a number of different occasions.

HL's carers decided to challenge the House of Lords ruling of 1998 and in October 2004 the European Court of Human Rights ruled that HL had been illegally detained. Whereas the House of Lords had considered the issue of unlawful detention under English common law (doctrine of necessity), the ECHR considered HL's case in relation to Article 5 of the Human Rights Act and found that he had been illegally deprived of his liberty as he and his carers had no right of appeal; the absence of procedural safeguards and access to a court was found to be a breach of Article 5(1) and 5(4).

Although the details of this case are well known now to those working in the mental health field, it is worth reiterating them here to provide the background context for the DOLS. Bournewood set the scene for respecting the rights of vulnerable people who would not necessarily meet the criteria for detention under the Mental Health Act but who nevertheless were in situations that amounted to confinement. The very fact that the DOLS were designed to plug a gap in the law may have some bearing on their perceived failure to date to be properly understood and applied, as this is a law that was devised in a rush and has not yet had time to evolve. Some commentators such as Richard Jones have argued that amending the existing law around guardianship under the Mental Health Act would have been a better way of providing such protection as opposed to introducing a very complicated new piece of law. Jones (2012) remains critical of the safeguards, referring to them as *a mess comprising impenetrable law that provides minimal rights for P and P's carers at considerable cost to the public purse* (Preface to *MCA Manual*, 5th edition).

However, while many experts agree with the bulk of the criticisms, some commentators have provided coherent arguments as to why amendments to guardianship would not have been sufficient. Series (2012), for example, has noted that while guardianship offers some protection of the rights of individuals, it shares a number of weaknesses of the DOLS regime, including the fact that neither regime has an answer to the problem of widespread, de facto unlawful detention. As it stands, there is no clear duty on anybody to seek the authority of a guardian, whereas the DOLS regime at least spells out a requirement for relevant care settings to seek authority from a supervisory body should they become aware of a potential deprivation.

Definitions of deprivation: the Human Rights and Mental Capacity Acts

As indicated by the ruling in Bournewood, the DOLS are inextricably bound up with the Human Rights Act 1998, in particular Article 5, the right to liberty, and Article 8, the right to respect for private and family life. When working with service users such as Rosemary (see pages 4–6), and making decisions about care and treatment and where this should be provided, both articles come into play within the hospital setting and in any proposed 24-hour placement. The Deprivation of Liberty Safeguards are designed to allow practitioners to make decisions for people like Rosemary in their best interests, but to provide a legal umbrella or safeguard so that their rights are considered and respected; and most fundamentally there is a mechanism for appeal. This appeal mechanism is provided by the role of the representative, which we will explore later in the chapter.

This all seems relatively straightforward until we consider that the DOLS were introduced as an addition to the Mental Capacity Act 2005. The link here is again fundamental in that the DOLS only apply to those who have been assessed as lacking capacity to consent to their care and treatment, but discrepancies can occur when considering what might be a restriction on liberty as sanctioned by section 6 of the MCA and what is, in fact, a deprivation of liberty. The Mental Capacity Act clearly allows health and social care professionals to make decisions on behalf of those who lack capacity to consent to care and treatment in their best interests and to use restraint in order to do this, provided that it is necessary to prevent a person coming to harm and that the restraint is a proportionate response to the likelihood of a person suffering serious harm (see MCA *Code of Practice*). Examples of restraints or restrictions that can occur in a person's care include environmental, physical, chemical, levels of observation, one-to-one staffing, restrictions on access to the community, contact and discharge.

Activity 6.1

Consider Rosemary's case again and make a list of the different restrictions on her liberty while she is in hospital. In particular, consider her inability to move around and the medications that may be used to subdue her agitation.

Comment

See the following list for possible restrictions you should have identified.

- *Environmental: being nursed in isolation*
- *One-to-one staffing for personal care*
- *Low-level physical restraints when Rosemary lashes out*
- *Discharge restrictions*
- *Being unable to move without assistance of others*
- *Possible chemical restrictions – e.g. sedating medications*
- *Lack of access to community.*

Principle 6 of the MCA

Before the act is done, or the decision made, regard must be had to whether the purpose for which it is needed can be effectively achieved in a way that is less restrictive of the person's rights and freedom of action.

This principle is fundamental to all decisions and action that professionals take when working with adults who have been assessed as lacking capacity to consent to care and treatment. As such, this is no different when applying the Deprivation of Liberty Safeguards. For Rosemary, it might mean considering whether time-limited home visits might be in her best interests while she is in hospital or whether there are ways of calming her agitation on the ward without resorting to chemical sedation.

Under the safeguards, the best interests assessor is tasked with identifying first whether a deprivation of liberty is occurring and second whether such a deprivation is in the person's best interests. Until March 2014, when there was a landmark ruling from the Supreme Court (see Significant case law section, pages 96–7), there was a tendency to look at deprivation and define it by identifying restrictions in a person's care and then decide whether the intensity, frequency and duration of such restrictions amounted to a deprivation of liberty. This is the approach recommended by the DOLS *Code of Practice* (Department of Health, 2008a) and by case law until the Cheshire West judgment.

The wide national discrepancies in the use and application of the DOLS, as reported by the House of Lords and others, have a variety of causes. However, there must be some foundation for the discrepancy in this tension between those who see liberty as something that is lost incrementally through increased restrictions on an ongoing basis and those who see liberty as an absolute, which is immediately surrendered and compromised the moment an incapacitous person enters a 24-hour placement. The two approaches do not have to be mutually exclusive, but the writer would argue that the now blanket approach to identifying deprivation may have unintended consequences – namely, that by affording everyone the right of appeal, opportunities to recognise and encourage empowerment, supported decision making and choice within 24-hour care may be lost. By automatically assuming that an individual is deprived of their liberty, there is less room for recognising different models of care and treatment, and supporting those models that sit well within the ethos of the MCA.

What is liberty?

This is, of course, a question that is far too large and wide-ranging to answer in a social work textbook, but needs some reflection when considering concepts around deprivation of liberty.

Philosophers, writers, anti-slavery campaigners and politicians have grappled with this question over the centuries. As human society has evolved, the variety of ways in which liberty can be perceived has also changed. For example, there is currently a debate around the ability of governments and/or businesses to spy on civilians by means of mass electronic surveillance, as highlighted by the Wikileaks whistleblower, Julian Assange. Privacy and liberty are now closely linked in a way that historical commentators would not have considered. John Stuart Mill wrote his famous treatise *On Liberty* in 1859 and in this asserts:

> The only purpose for which power can be rightfully exercised over any member of a civilised community, 'against his will is to prevent harm to others. His own good either physical or moral', is not a sufficient warrant.

(Mill, 1909, p258)

John Stuart Mill argues for the rights of the individual over the powers of government and society as a whole and believes that ultimately society benefits more from allowing individuals to express themselves through opinion or action than if individuals are forced to conform to societal norms and rules. While Mill concedes that the individual must be prevented from harming others, he does not include in his treatise reference to vulnerable people with disabilities and the powers society should have in these circumstances, nor does he provide a definition of harm to others and the extent to which intervention can be justified. It is interesting to note that the rights of the individual as favoured by Mill still have strong political credence today and that these are argued for in the name of individual liberty, despite the fact we may all have far less freedom now than we like to think we have.

Activity 6.2

Think about how you would define your own liberty. In particular, list those aspects (for example, freedom to decide where you live) that you would not want to lose. Second, try to list factors in your life or environment that impinge on that liberty. How far does your second list represent everyday limitations that you are prepared to accept and how far does it represent loss of liberty? How would these lists change if you were diagnosed with dementia or suffered a serious physical or brain injury?

Comment

While Activity 6.2 may leave you feeling that the concept of liberty in different situations is necessarily hypothetical, these are some of the debates that have informed the development of the law around deprivation of liberty. For example, in the Cheshire West case, in the original ruling in 2011, Lord Justice Munby had advocated that a comparative approach should be taken when considering what was or was not deprivation of liberty. Munby suggested that a person who had severe dementia or learning disabilities could not expect the same degree of liberty as the average person on the street.

This approach was rightly identified as being discriminatory towards those with disabilities and has been completely overturned by the verdict of the Supreme Court in March 2014. Lady Hale commented that she found it *axiomatic that people with disabilities, both mental and physical, have the same human rights as the rest of the human race. It may be that those rights have sometimes to be limited or restricted because of their disabilities, but the starting point should be the same as for everyone else* (P *(by his litigation friend the Official Solicitor) v Cheshire West and Chester Council & Anor* [2014], paragraph 45).

The comparator approach, as it was known, was indeed discriminatory and caused further difficulties in the understanding and application of the safeguards, but in defence of Munby, there was a common-sense element to his reasoning. An older person in the last stages of dementia will lose the ability to speak, move, feed themselves and/or even swallow. This is not as a result of restrictions imposed on them, but a part of a progressive condition. Does the fact that they have to receive intensive and invasive 24-hour nursing care often in bed render them 'deprived of their liberty'? As the law now stands, the answer is 'yes', but many practitioners struggle with this concept, believing that this extra safeguard is an additional bureaucratic burden without any meaning for the person concerned. There are also unresolved questions over whether people in comas in hospital settings should be assessed under the DOLS:

> It seems particularly odd to think of the unconscious hospital patient receiving life-sustaining treatment as deprived of their liberty, but that may be the consequence of this decision.
>
> (*39 Essex Street Newsletter*, April 2014, p13)

Deprivation of liberty in other contexts

The concept of deprivation of liberty does not only exist in relation to health and social care settings, and legal debates around civil liberties are to be found in other contexts, such as the right to protest and terrorism cases where there are arguments about tagging and curfews in respect of suspects. Until case law relating to DOLS started to develop, courts looked to examples from other areas of law for guidance on the timescale and amount of restriction that might constitute deprivation of liberty. Examples were found in anti-terrorism legislation and the use of control orders, as well as in cases where state authorities such as the police restricted the liberty of people significantly.

In the case of Austin (*Austin v UK* [2012]), it was found that a group of protesters who had been held in a police cordon for eight hours – or 'kettled' – had not had their Article 5 rights breached as the police had acted in a pragmatic way that did not equate to arbitrary detention. There were dissenting voices in this judgment, demonstrating how the concept of liberty can be very much a political as well as a philosophical and legal one.

The DOLS as they stand currently only apply to people who reside in registered hospitals and care homes. This does not mean that deprivation of liberty cannot occur in other settings such as supported living or domestic settings, and the law requires that the Court of Protection is approached to authorise deprivation in those situations. The duty to do this is placed on either the supported living provider or on the local authority. This duty was not always fully recognised until the Supreme Court ruling in March 2014, which also considered the cases of Mig and Meg (see pages 97–8), who were two sisters with learning disabilities, one residing in a domestic foster care setting, and found that they too were deprived of their liberty. Local authorities are now actively trying to identify cases they need to take to the Court of Protection for authorisation, resulting in further delays for hearings in the courts.

Significant case law

In the discussions above, we have made a number of references to significant cases, in particular the Cheshire West case. As this case has had a profound impact on the law to date, we will discuss it in detail first and then look at providing references to other cases that have influenced the understanding and application of the DOLS.

Cheshire West

This case concerned a 39-year-old man, P, with cerebral palsy, Down's syndrome, and learning and physical disabilities. P had been moved to Z House, a spacious bungalow accommodating up to four residents in 2009, from his mother's house after a deterioration in her health and a reduction in her ability to care for P. P attended a day centre five days a week and was supervised by staff when he was there; he was also supervised closely within Z House due to his tendency to display challenging behaviours. P used a wheelchair and needed one-to-one support with his personal care. One of P's challenging behaviours involved shredding his incontinence pads, smearing faeces and ingesting the pads. As a result, a care plan was put in place for P to wear an all-in-one body suit with the fastenings at the back to prevent P from having access to his pads. P's mother supported the placement, and family contact was maintained and encouraged. The fact that the care plans for P were in his best interests was never in dispute; the legal debate hinged on whether the care arrangements were or were not a deprivation of liberty.

In 2011 this case was heard at the Court of Appeal and Lord Justice Munby concluded that P was not deprived of his liberty. (In 2009 a judge had found that it was deprivation.) Munby considered relevant case law at the time but went on to analyse the information in terms of 'context, reason, purpose and motive'. As cited earlier, Munby felt that the reasons and purpose for a placement were relevant for defining deprivation, as was comparing like with like: he did not feel the restrictions placed on P and the loss of liberty relating to this should be equated with the average person without disabilities and the liberty they expected to enjoy. The 'relative normality' of any situation needed to be considered before concluding there was a deprivation of liberty.

This judgment has now been overturned by the Supreme Court, but did at the time lead to further confusion and misunderstanding of where the safeguards applied; in particular, confusion arose where assessors saw that care and treatment arrangements for an individual were in their best interests and so concluded there was no deprivation.

Supreme Court ruling 2014

The Supreme Court revisited Lord Justice Munby's judgment of 2011 and completely overturned it, concluding that P had been deprived of his liberty at Z House; it rejected the idea that the purpose of a placement was relevant and dismissed the idea that assessors or the courts should consider a comparator when weighing up whether there was deprivation or not. Lady Hale and the other judges agreed on a list of factors they considered were not relevant when deciding whether someone was deprived of their liberty or not:

> *The person's compliance or lack of objection is not relevant; the relative normality of the placement (whatever the comparison made) is not relevant; and the reason or purpose behind a particular placement is also not relevant.*

(paragraph 50)

Acid test

This ruling also issued what is now known as the 'acid test' for ascertaining whether there is deprivation or not in a case – namely, *that the person is not free to leave and is subject to continuous supervision and control*. Both of these criteria have to be met. While there is now general consensus that most people who lack capacity to consent to residing in a 24-hour placement will not be 'free to leave' – i.e. they would be prevented from discharging themselves if they tried to do so – there is still some uncertainty and debate about what amounts to continuous supervision and control. This aspect of the acid test was considered in relation to the cases of Mig and Meg, which were also incorporated into the appeal heard by the Supreme Court.

Mig and Meg

This case concerned two sisters who became subject to care proceedings in 2007 when they were aged 15 and 16; both had learning disabilities. Mig was placed with a foster mother and attended further education daily with an escort; she never attempted to leave by herself but would have been restrained if she had tried to do so. Meg was moved to a residential placement for people with learning difficulties and complex needs and, in addition to support and supervision, sometimes needed physical restraints and sedating medications. In 2009, Judge J Parker had concluded that neither sister was deprived of her liberty, but in the Supreme Court ruling of March 2014, this was overturned:

> *If the acid test is whether someone is under complete supervision and control of those caring for her and is not free to leave the place where she lives, then the truth is that both Mig and Meg are being deprived of their liberty.*

> (Lady Hale, paragraph 54)

Lady Hale went on to comment that the extreme vulnerability of people such as P, Mig and Meg made it necessary to err on the side of caution when deciding on whether there is deprivation or not. This link between vulnerability and the use of the DOLS is highly pertinent for all those practising in health and social care.

London Borough of Hillingdon v Steven Neary and Ors [2011]

While to date we have focused in some detail on recent case law that has debated and refined a definition of deprivation, it is worth considering a case where the focus is more about whether deprivation is in a person's best interests or not.

Steven Neary was a young man with autism who usually resided with his father, his main carer. Steven was admitted to respite care one Christmas with his father's agreement but then Hillingdon Social Services decided to keep him longer on the basis of concern as to whether Steven could be cared for at home, mainly due to Steven's weight. Hillingdon refused to allow Steven to return home despite his father requesting this and Steven expressing a consistent wish to do so. No DOLS authorisations were put in place until Steven had been in 24-hour care for four months and, when the safeguards were eventually used, the conclusion was that it was in Steven's best interests to stay there without even considering the possibility of him returning home. When the case did eventually get to court some ten months later, it was decided that Steven had been unlawfully deprived of his liberty and that he should be allowed to return home. There were a number of criticisms by the judge (Mr Justice Peter Jackson) of both the local authority and the best interests assessments. These included the fact that Hillingdon failed to bring the case before the Court of Protection, failed to appoint an IMCA and failed to conduct effective reviews of the DOLS authorisation. In particular the best interests assessors were criticised for not appointing Steven's father as his representative, therefore not enabling him to appeal the deprivation, and for taking the party line of the local authority without giving the case proper independent scrutiny.

Mr Justice Peter Jackson commented: *In this case, far from being a safeguard, the way in which the DOL process was used masked the real deprivation of liberty, which was the refusal to allow Steven to go home.*

There was a view that because the best interests assessors were also employed by Hillingdon, they had not acted independently enough. One of the main impacts of this case on the practice of DOLS has been for the onus to be shifted to the local authority to take disputed cases to the Court of Protection. Before Neary, there was an understanding that the appeal process rested with the person appointed as representative and that they should then bring the case before the court. Steven's father, however, faced many obstacles before he was able to challenge the DOLS: he struggled to find expert legal advice, initially he was not given the role of representative and, when he was, he was not offered the support of an IMCA. As a result of the difficulties, it is now recognised that the local authority should take the lead in referring disputed cases to the Court of Protection and that any person appointed as representative for someone under a deprivation of liberty should be offered the support of an IMCA.

The other important learning point from this case is that the safeguards should not be used as a way of enforcing a limited view of a person's best interests:

> The DOL safeguard should not be used by a local authority as a means of getting its own way on the question of whether it is in the person's best interests to be in the place at all.

> (Mr Justice Peter Jackson)

Interface between the Mental Health Act (amended) and Deprivation of Liberty Safeguards

At times when vulnerable adults are in psychiatric hospitals for treatment, it is not always clear which legal framework should be used – i.e. should they be detained under section 2 or section 3 of the Mental Health Act, or should a DOLS authorisation be implemented? There has been case law that attempts to define this and we will cite these for further reading. In essence, however, the current position is that if a person with identified mental health problems is clearly objecting to treatment within a psychiatric hospital, then mental health legislation should be applied as opposed to the DOLS. (See *Northamptonshire Healthcare NHS Foundation Trust & Anor v ML (Rev 1)* [2014])

Case law has also suggested that professionals should consider which is the least restrictive regime for an individual. (*AM v South London and Maudsley NHS Foundation Trust and others* [2013]). Such a distinction is not always clear as some might feel there is less stigma attached to a DOLS authorisation than being 'sectioned' and there are potential differences between which regime offers the most robust appeal process. For example, if Rosemary was subject to section 2 of the Mental Health Act, potentially she could challenge her detention within 14 days of her admission, whereas under the DOLS she could wait a lot longer for her case to be heard at the Court of Protection and this would depend on her representative or the local authority making this challenge for her. Equally if a person is detained under section 3 when in hospital, they then become automatically entitled to section 117 aftercare, which means they will not be expected to pay for future care, for example in a residential setting. No such entitlement exists with a DOLS authorisation. The interaction between these two pieces of law is complex and even lawyers admit to much head scratching with it, but as a social worker you just need to be aware that there are ongoing debates around this subject. The new Mental Health Act *Code of Practice* also has useful guidance and a flowchart to help professionals decide which piece of law should be used.

Deprivation of Liberty Safeguards in practice

In the first half of this chapter, we have discussed how and why the DOLS came into force and some of the tensions inherent within them, from both a legal and philosophical perspective. We have also provided a summary and analysis of significant case law, which practitioners should be aware of when considering how and when the safeguards should apply. In this section we will explore how the safeguards work in practice.

If you have felt slightly confused to date by what a deprivation of liberty is, it may help to envisage the safeguard as a legal umbrella that sits over an individual's care and treatment. This umbrella does not necessarily change the care and treatment a person receives or how that person receives it, but it does represent a recognition of the circumstances and offers a right of appeal once it is in place. In order for a deprivation of liberty to be authorised (or sanctioned) in a person's best interests, there is a process (of a very bureaucratic nature) that needs to take place. It is necessary to understand the definitions below to be able to follow the process.

> **Managing authority**: The hospital or registered care home where the person is residing.
>
> **Supervisory body**: The local authority which is responsible for funding the person's care or would be responsible for the person, where they are in receipt of health-funded care and treatment or are self-funding.
>
> **Best interests assessor**: A professional (social worker, occupational therapist, psychologist, nurse), who has undertaken the relevant specialist training to undertake this role in relation to the DOLS.
>
> **Mental health assessor**: A doctor approved under section 12 of the Mental Health Act, who has undertaken the necessary training to complete assessments for the DOLS.
>
> **Conditions**: Recommendations that may be attached to any deprivation of liberty authorisation. These recommendations are legally binding, but need to relate either to enforcing the deprivation of liberty or reducing the need for it in future.
>
> **Representative**: A family member or friend of the person or, in the absence of an appropriate person, an IMCA, who is appointed to represent the person and who has a right of appeal over the person's care and treatment.

Reviews: These are conducted when a DOLS authorisation is about to expire depending on the timescales set for it or when there are significant changes to a person's care and treatment. Another DOLS authorisation can then be put in place if needed.

Roles and responsibilities

The managing authority

By law the hospital or care home where the person is has a duty to identify whether the care and treatment it is providing to an individual might be a deprivation of liberty and, if so, make a referral for that person to be formally assessed. A senior member of staff would then have responsibility to complete two forms known as an 'urgent authorisation' (form 1) and a standard request (form 4). These have to be forwarded immediately to the supervisory body.

The urgent authorisation in effect is the care home or hospital giving itself legal permission to deprive a person of their liberty for seven days until the formal assessments are carried out by the best interests assessor and mental health assessor. The standard request (form 4) also has to be completed at the same time. If there are circumstances where managing authorities identify in advance that they will need to use DOLS, then a standard request can be submitted beforehand and allows 21 days for the assessments to take place.

In reality, the huge upsurge in referrals (33,000 requests between March and October 2014) following the Cheshire West judgment in March 2014 has resulted in the statutory timescales being lost as requests for assessments are being stacked. This has potentially serious consequences for people's rights as there is often a long delay in the assessments taking place and the safeguards being effectively implemented. Note: There is no automatic right of appeal unless a deprivation of liberty is formally authorised in a person's best interests.

The managing authority also has a legal responsibility to ensure that any conditions attached to an authorisation for a person in their care are met. Once a deprivation of liberty authorisation is granted for someone in their care, the managing authority has the responsibility to inform the person concerned, to notify the supervisory body of any changes to that person's care and treatment, and to request a review of the DOLS authorisation when necessary.

The supervisory body

The supervisory body has the responsibility to receive referrals from the managing authorities and then commission the relevant assessments from best interests assessors and mental health assessors. Most local authorities have arrangements in place to train assessors or to commission such training, but before the changes in March 2014, some supervisory bodies were contracting solely with independent assessors or through agencies. Given the huge increase in demand for DOLS assessments, there is a rush to train increasing numbers of assessors to meet the demand:

> *Unsurprisingly almost every local authority who responded to our FOI request is looking to boost BIA numbers. This is not, however, easy. Training a BIA is costly.*

(McNicoll, 2014)

The supervisory body has responsibility for scrutinising the assessments it receives from the best interests and mental health assessors and then to authorise these if they satisfy the requirements (see below). This scrutiny and authorisation are usually undertaken by a senior manager or a panel of managers, who ultimately have the responsibility for 'signing off' or authorising the deprivation of liberty. Where best interests assessors are employed direct by the local authority, which is also the supervisory body, there are some concerns that this may lead to a conflict of interest or a tendency for the supervisory body to rubber stamp existing decisions – see details of the Neary case on pages 98–9.

Other responsibilities include collating all the information and issuing the standard authorisations and making sure that all relevant individuals who have been consulted as part of the assessment receive a copy of the paperwork. One of the most important duties for the supervisory body is that of appointing an IMCA (see Chapter 3) for the person who becomes subject to a DOLS authorisation. There are three different types of IMCA that can be appointed in relation to the DOLS depending on the function that the law requires them to perform.

- 39(a) If, when an urgent authorisation is issued, there is no one available to consult in terms of family or friend, then the supervisory body needs to appoint an IMCA so that the best interests assessor can consult with them as part of the initial assessment.

- 39(c) Once the best interests assessor has decided that a deprivation of liberty is occurring in a person's best interests, then they have a duty to appoint a representative for that person. If there is no suitable family or friend available, then the supervisory body has to appoint an IMCA to this position.

- 39(d) It is now recommended practice for every representative appointed who is a family member or friend to have an IMCA assigned to them so that they have the support of an individual who understands the law and appeal process if they want this.

Supervisory bodies bear the burden of the bureaucracy that bedevils the DOLS process and they require dedicated teams to work through the legal processes and ensure that all the paperwork is issued in a correct and timely manner. Supervisory bodies also ultimately carry legal liability for ensuring that people are not deprived of their liberty unlawfully in their area. This said, if care homes and hospitals do not ask for these assessments by issuing urgent authorisations, then it is hard to see how local authorities can be held accountable. It is interesting to note that there were no DOLS authorisations in place at the Winterbourne care home, suggesting that the most vulnerable did not receive this safeguard as the care home did not ask for this.

There is a provision in the regulations that allows a member of the public or professional to report unauthorised deprivations of liberty to the relevant supervisory body, but this is as yet not well known or widely utilised (DOLS *Code of Practice*, Department of Health, 2008a, p94).

Best interests and mental health assessors

These individuals have to undertake the necessary training for roles and are responsible for the six assessments that have to be completed for a DOLS authorisation. These individuals also have a professional duty to ensure that they keep their training up to date and keep abreast of all legal changes that occur. There is some overlap between roles and different areas divide the workload differently depending on their commissioning arrangements. The six assessments are as follows.

1. **Mental health assessment**: This assessment can only be done by the mental health assessor, who has to verify that an individual is suffering from a mental disorder as defined by the amended Mental Health Act 1983. If the doctor assigned decides that the person does not have a mental disorder, then all the assessments will stop and the person will not be eligible for the DOLS.

2. **Eligibility assessment**: This assessment can be undertaken either by the mental health assessor or by the best interests assessor if they are also trained as an AMHP (Approved Mental Health Professional under the amended Mental Health Act). This assessment serves the function of establishing whether a person should be detained under the Mental Health Act as opposed to under a DOLS authorisation. Ostensibly, this can be straightforward as if someone is already detained, under a section 2 or 3, this makes them ineligible for the DOLS. However, there has been legal confusion at times (see pages 99–100) over which law should have primacy. Equally, if a person is subject to a community treatment order or guardianship under the Mental Health Act, this does not automatically make him or her ineligible for DOLS, unless there is a conflict between the requirements of both sets of legislation.

3. **Capacity assessment**: This assessment can be done either by the mental health or best interests assessor and is necessary to establish whether the individual does or does not have capacity to reside in an establishment for the purposes of receiving care and treatment. See Chapter 4 for an analysis of how capacity assessments should be carried out.

   One of the challenges involved in a capacity assessment for the purposes of the DOLS is that when assessors are working within statutory timescales (only having three or four days to complete this piece of work), there is little time to try to support an individual with decision making. Equally, assessors are usually independent and have no knowledge of the person concerned other than what they are given by staff in the 24-hour placement. Note: it is important to remember that capacity assessments are always for specific decisions and the one in relation to the DOLS is quite broad in its remit. Where there are particular safeguarding aspects to a case – for example, concerns about an individual who may have been exploiting or neglecting a vulnerable adult – the DOLS capacity assessment can only really focus on the vulnerable adult's ability to understand their need for care and treatment in a 24-hour setting, not on their relationship with such an individual. This does not preclude separate capacity assessments being carried out around the relationship, and it would be good practice for these to be done.

If the mental health or best interests assessor concludes that a vulnerable adult does have capacity for the purposes of the DOLS, this can often present social workers and other professionals with a sudden challenge, especially if their service user is demanding to leave a 24-hour placement and return home immediately. Once an individual is deemed to have capacity, no decisions can be made for him or her and the legal process stops. In these circumstances it would be good practice for the best interests or mental health assessor to talk to the service user about agreeing to stay where they are for a few more days to allow services at home to be put in place if necessary. Alternatively, if there are serious concerns about the outcome of the capacity assessment, then the supervisory body can recommission the assessment and obtain a second opinion or refer to the Court of Protection for a ruling on capacity (see Chapter 4).

4. **No refusals assessment**: This assessment has to be undertaken by the best interests assessor and serves the purpose of identifying if there are any legal obstacles in terms of advance decisions, LPAs or deputies for health and welfare, which would not allow the DOLS authorisation to go ahead. The existence of someone appointed as LPA or deputy for health and welfare decisions who disagrees about care and treatment arrangements, or a clear advance decision refusing a specific proposed treatment, would trump the legal authority of DOLS and thus an authorisation could not go ahead. It is worth noting that many relatives do make arrangements to take responsibility for a loved one's financial affairs, but fewer have legal authority to make health and welfare decisions; if a relative or friend does have such powers and is in full agreement with the care and treatment arrangements, then the authorisation goes ahead.

On rare occasions there may be problems where the best interests assessor identifies that a person who poses a known safeguarding risk to a vulnerable adult also holds an LPA or deputyship for health and welfare decisions for the adult. The first task of the best interests assessor or you as social worker would be to establish if such a power is valid and has been registered with the Office of the Public Guardian. If it is and there is a clear risk that a vulnerable adult will come to harm if the DOLS is not authorised, swift action needs to be taken to challenge the individual's role in the Court of Protection. Any deputy or attorney has to act in a person's best interests and if they are not doing so, then this needs a legal challenge before they can be divested of these responsibilities.

5. **Age assessment**: This is completed by the best interests assessor and is purely to verify whether the person is 18 years or above. It is worth noting that the Mental Capacity Act applies to people aged 16 and above, whereas to be eligible for a DOLS authorisation you need to be 18. This discrepancy can catch practitioners unawares, especially as the Mental Health Act applies to children as well as adults.

6. **Best interests assessment**: This is probably the most substantial piece of work out of the six qualifying assessments and, as its name suggests, is completed by the best interests assessor (BIA). The main purpose of this assessment is to establish first if a person is deprived of his or her liberty and secondly, if so, whether the deprivation of liberty is in the person's best interests. As part of this assessment, the BIA has also to be satisfied that the care and treatment arrangements are necessary to prevent the person coming to harm and that the arrangements are a proportionate response to the likelihood of the person suffering significant harm. If the BIA decides that any of these criteria are not met, then the DOLS authorisation does not go ahead. Note: if the BIA finds that a person is deprived but it is not in best interests, then care providers and commissioners are required to act promptly to change the person's care and treatment and/or placement.

In order to complete this assessment, the best interests assessor has to meet with the person and interview them, study all their care plans and discuss these with the managing authority and then consult with all relevant people before completing a substantial piece of written work that needs to be of a high enough standard to stand up in court, should any case be referred to the Court of Protection. It is estimated that doing such a piece of work can take up to ten hours or more depending on the complexity of the case. In the 2011 Neary case (see pages 98–9), Mr Justice Peter Jackson commented that the written best interests assessment is *anything but a routine piece of paperwork. Properly viewed, it should be seen as a cornerstone of the protection that the DOL safeguards offer to people.*

The best interests assessor also has the responsibility of identifying a representative for a person who lacks capacity to choose this person for themselves, and recommending such a person to the supervisory body. The best interests assessor recommends how long an authorisation should last (anywhere between 14 days and a year) and can specify conditions to which the DOL needs to be subject.

We will address some of the challenges the best interests assessor faces in their role at the end of the chapter, particularly in relation to safeguarding issues, but first test out your knowledge with the following questions.

Activity 6.3

1. Who is responsible for making a request for a DOLS assessment?

   A. The best interests assessor
   B. The supervisory body (local authority)
   C. The managing authority (care home/hospital)

2. Who can exercise the right of appeal over a DOLS authorisation?

   A. The person themselves
   B. The appointed representative and/or IMCA
   C. The supervisory body

3. Who authorises the deprivation of liberty?

   A. The best interests assessor
   B. The mental health assessor
   C. The supervisory body

4. The DOLS as the law stands apply:

   A. Everywhere
   B. In registered care homes, hospitals and supported living placements
   C. Only in registered care home and hospital settings

5. Who can complete the capacity assessment for the DOLS?

   A. Only the best interests assessor
   B. Only the mental health assessor
   C. Both the above.

Comment

For answers to Activity 6.3, see the end of this chapter.

DOLS and safeguarding

As indicated throughout this chapter, there were fundamental problems until March 2014 in identifying and defining deprivation of liberty. While there are still difficulties in applying the new acid test – for example, intensive care units are struggling with the concept of the potential need for DOLS authorisations at the same time as trying to perform life-saving treatment – there is now less room for disagreement in terms of a definition. What does remain, however, is often a conflict between the desire to protect vulnerable individuals and how far the DOLS can be used for this purpose.

There can be a tendency to conflate fear of a vulnerable person coming to harm with trying to use the DOLS as a blunt tool to force someone to remain in 24-hour care for protection. This is particularly evident where an individual's capacity to consent to care is borderline and they may well have capacity to choose to return to a situation about which professionals have concerns. In such cases, both the BIA and the mental health assessor need to be vigilant that a thorough capacity assessment is completed and the DOLS assessment results in upholding an individual's Article 5 and 8 rights as opposed to being used purely as a legal holding power for the professionals' ease of mind. As highlighted in Chapter 5, any situations where there is ongoing dispute between family members or where there is a breach of Article 8 will need to be referred to the Court of Protection in addition to any DOLS authorisation that is put in place. Where a vulnerable adult is found to have capacity to decide where to live, but there remain significant safeguarding concerns, then professionals need to approach their legal departments to seek advice about whether the High Court can be approached, possibly to use injunctions against known abusers.

DOLS authorisations are often in place to protect individuals – for example, stopping an older person with memory loss from wandering out at night or on to a busy road, but the purpose of the assessments must be to look at the least restrictive way of achieving this care and treatment with a strong emphasis on respecting the person's human rights. The BIA has to find a balance between the need to prevent an individual coming to harm and respect for their rights, wishes and feelings in the same way that professionals are required to make best interests decisions (see Chapter 5). Frequently, BIAs will use conditions attached to authorisations to try to achieve this balance for a vulnerable person. For example, where an individual with severe memory loss is repeatedly trying to leave a locked environment, the BIA may specify that the care staff take the person out for a walk on a regular basis to try to alleviate this distress and reduce the deprivation they are experiencing.

As highlighted throughout this book, the interface between the MCA/DOLS and safeguarding concerns is not straightforward and professionals need to be capable of working with complexity in situations, where it is not always possible to find a 'right' or 'wrong' answer. The art of balancing the need to protect an individual from harm while upholding their rights is an essential skill for those who train as best interests assessors.

Activity 6.4

Return to the case study for Rosemary (pages 4–6) and apply what you have learned from your reading to the following questions:

1. What is the deprivation of liberty authorising?
2. If you and others disagree with the conditions attached, are you legally obliged to comply with them?
3. Do you still need to go ahead with your own best interests meeting?
4. What will happen when the DOLS authorisation runs out?

Comment

Potential answers are as follows.

1. *Hopefully, you have identified that the DOL is a recognition of the fact that Rosemary is not free to leave the ward and that she is under the continuous supervision and control of nursing staff and that this is in her best interests for an eight-week period while longer term plans are made for her care and treatment.*
2. *The short answer is yes, conditions are legally binding. However, if it is impossible to get the care package you need for trial leave or if Rosemary returned home and care broke down, then she could be returned to the ward environment. You as social worker and the ward staff will need to demonstrate that you have made every effort to comply with the conditions.*
3. *The answer is yes as your roles and responsibilities under the MCA continue alongside the DOLS authorisation. It may be possible to delay your meeting as to such time as Rosemary has had further assessments either at home or in hospital so as to have more information available with which to reach a decision (see Chapter 5).*
4. *Either Rosemary will go home or if she needs to remain longer in hospital a review of the authorisation will be carried out and a further DOLS authorisation put in place.*

Becoming a social worker

If you have not trained as a BIA, you may feel that the intricacies and complexities of the DOLS legislation can be left to those who have. However, as a social worker you will increasingly be coming across situations where DOLS authorisations are in place for your service users and you need to be aware of how the law works and your responsibilities in relation to this.

In particular you need to be aware that your role as social worker continues in relation to best interests decision making for service users alongside any DOLS authorisations and that you retain professional responsibility for decision making, but at the same time paying heed to what an independent BIA has concluded or recommended. If you are newly qualified and unsure of your role in such situations, seeking supervision from an experienced practitioner is fundamental.

In addition to supervision, it may help you to shadow a best interests assessor for an assessment to gain a clear understanding of their role. If you wish to consider training as a BIA you will need to have two years' post-qualifying experience and will then need to be released to take a short Masters-level course at a university which offers the training.

Chapter Summary

The Deprivation of Liberty Safeguards remain a complex piece of law but if applied thoroughly can be a vital safeguard for the rights of vulnerable individuals. We have highlighted some of the reasons why historically these safeguards have not always been properly understood or applied, but would argue that the current law (or at least something very similar following the proposed changes in 2018) is likely to remain part of the social and healthcare landscape. Social work has had a long tradition of advocating for people's human rights and as such we need to recognise and embrace the DOLS as a tool to support us in this process.

Further Reading

The Care Quality Commission (www.cqc.org.uk) is now tasked with monitoring the use of the DOLS regulations via its inspection regimes. For up-to-date overviews, see its annual reports.

Both Houses of Parliament have recently scrutinised the operation and impact of mental health and mental capacity legislation, including the DOLS.

The two reports which emerged from this scrutiny are very revealing and their comments in relation to DOLS are worth scrutinising.

House of Commons Health Committee (2013) *Post-legislative Scrutiny of the Mental Health Act 2007*, paras 106–7. London: The Stationery Office.

House of Lords Select Committee on the Mental Capacity Act 2005 (2014) *Mental Capacity Act 2005: Post-legislative scrutiny*. London: The Stationery Office.

Answers to questions in Activity 6.3

Q1. Who is responsible for making a request for a DOLS assessment?

C. The managing authority (care home/hospital)

Q2. Who can exercise the right of appeal over a DOLS authorisation?

A. The person themselves

B. The appointed representative and/or IMCA

C. The supervisory body

Q3. Who authorises the deprivation of liberty?

C. The supervisory body

Q4. The DOLS as the law stands apply:

C. Only in registered care home and hospital settings

Q5. Who can complete the capacity assessment for the DOLS?

C. Both the mental health assessor and the best interests assessor.

Chapter 7

Adults at risk

Meeting professional standards

This chapter will help you to develop the following selected capabilities, to the appropriate level, from the social work Professional Capabilities Framework.

Professionalism

- Identify and implement strategies for responding appropriately to concerns about practice or procedures, seeking guidance if required.

Interventions and skills

- Use appropriate assessment frameworks, applying information-gathering skills to make and contribute to assessments, while continuing to build relationships and offer support.
- Select, use and review appropriate and timely social work interventions, informed by evidence of their effectiveness, that are best suited to the service user(s), family, carer, setting and self.
- Share information consistently in ways that meet legal, ethical and agency requirements.
- Demonstrate understanding of and respond to risk factors in your practice. Contribute to the assessment and management of risk, including strategies for reducing risk, distinguishing levels of risk for different situations.
- Demonstrate application of principles and practice for safeguarding adults and children including consideration of potential abuse. Apply strategies that aim to reduce and prevent harm and abuse.

Knowledge

- Understand forms of harm and their impact on people, and the implications for practice, drawing on concepts of strength, resilience, vulnerability, risk and resistance, and apply to practice.

Introduction

Since 2000 and the publication of the *No Secrets* guidance, local authorities have had a leading co-ordinating role with all relevant organisations on safeguarding adults in their geographical area. The Care Act 2014 put this role into primary legislation for the first time. This is in line with the general intention of the Act to consolidate adult social care legislation, and to bring into law a wide range of previous policy and guidance. Local authorities are required, under the Act, to develop new policies and procedures at local level to ensure the implementation of this legislation.

Protection from abuse and neglect and encouraging physical and mental health and emotional well-being are included in Part 1 of the Care Act as important general principles underpinning care and support for adults. However, the long-standing tension between safeguarding adults and promoting their autonomy and independence is continued, as other general principles include maintaining personal dignity, treating individuals with respect, and control by the individual over their day-to-day life. In an ideal world, these principles would not be in conflict, but such a world would have little need of social workers. We spend most of our working lives deciding what weight to give to each of these principles in complex situations where there is no clear-cut answer.

This chapter aims to equip you to carry out your safeguarding duties lawfully and professionally, in the context of legislation relating to mental capacity.

In the Care Act 2014, safeguarding is one of six themes workers are expected to consider at each stage of the process of assessment of need, and eligibility for local authority funding. The other five are mental capacity, advocacy and participation support, the impact on family and carers, a strengths-based approach, and a response which is proportionate and appropriate. An assessment or review can trigger a safeguarding enquiry or vice versa, and risk as well as need must be considered at assessment and review. The safeguarding duty is independent of the assessment duty and while it may arise within an assessment or lead to it, it will often be exercised completely separately.

The Act sets six principles for work aimed at safeguarding adults:

- **empowerment** – presumption of person-led decisions and informed consent;

- **prevention** – it is better to take action before harm comes;

- **proportionality** – proportionate and least intrusive response appropriate to the risk presented;

- **protection** – support and representation for those in greatest need;

- **partnerships** – local solutions through services working with their communities;

- **accountability** – accountability and transparency in delivering safeguarding.

From April 2015 each local authority must:

- make enquiries, or ensure others do so, if it believes that an adult is subject to, or at risk of, abuse or neglect;

- set up a Safeguarding Adults Board with core membership from the local authority, the police and the NHS (specifically the local Clinical Commissioning Group/s) and the power to include other relevant bodies;

- arrange, where appropriate, for an independent advocate to represent and support an adult who is the subject of a safeguarding enquiry or a Safeguarding Adult Review where the adult has 'substantial difficulty' in being involved in the process and where there is no other appropriate adult to help them.

The key responsibility for adult safeguarding is with local authorities in partnership with the police and the NHS, and these three form the core membership of Safeguarding Adults Boards. Issues concerning the configuration and role of these boards are included in Chapter 8, where we will look at the interaction of the wide range of agencies who may be involved in the care and support of adults with and without capacity. Here, we focus on the duties placed on the local authority to ensure safeguarding enquiries are made when required and to arrange advocacy when necessary.

Care Act 2014 section 42: duty to make enquiries

The local authority must ensure that enquiries are made where it has reasonable cause to suspect that an adult in its area (whether or not ordinarily resident there):

- has needs for care and support (whether or not these are being met, by the local authority or anyone else);

- is experiencing, or is at risk of, abuse or neglect; and

- as a result of those needs is unable to protect himself or herself against the abuse or neglect or the risk of it.

Despite the changing terminology, from vulnerable adult through adult at risk to adult with care and support needs, this remains close in meaning to the definition in the *No Secrets* guidance (Department of Health, 2000), where a vulnerable adult is someone *who is or may be in need of community care services by reason of mental or other disability, age or illness; and who is or may be unable to take care of him or herself, or unable to protect him or herself against significant harm or exploitation* (para. 2.3).

The emphasis now is on care and support needs, rather than on the person's need for services. The local authority has a duty to make a safeguarding enquiry even if their needs are unmet, perhaps because they are not at the level of eligibility where local authority provision can be made or because the person may be able to afford to pay for it themselves.

In the Care Act section 42, 'adult' refers to someone who is 18 or older. This does not correlate with other relevant legislation, particularly that which relates to consent to medical treatment, sexual activity and some financial accountabilities. Entitlements to benefits, education and support from provision through children's services also have varying age requirements.

Having a disability or being old and frail does not automatically make someone unable to make decisions or vulnerable, but they may come to be at risk of abuse or neglect because of ill health, disability, getting older, social or geographical isolation, or inappropriate accommodation. An adult with care and support needs may be an older person, a person with a physical disability, a learning disability or a sensory impairment, someone with mental health needs, including dementia or a personality disorder, a person with a long-term health condition, or someone who misuses substances or alcohol to the extent that it affects their ability to manage day-to-day living.

This is not an exhaustive list: the legislation also includes people who are victims of sexual exploitation, domestic abuse and modern slavery. Where there is a potential criminal offence, safeguarding is not an alternative to police involvement and would only be applicable at all where a person has care and support needs that mean that they are not able to protect themselves.

Safeguarding duties apply to people who pay for their own care and support services. The financial assessment should follow the assessment of needs and eligibility and local authorities must tell people that they can ask the authority to meet their needs, even if the person's resources mean that they will pay the full cost. If the local authority believes the individual may lack capacity, it should check whether someone else is dealing with their affairs (for instance, a Lasting Power of Attorney) and if there is, they must be consulted.

Adult safeguarding duties apply in all settings where people live, with the exception of prisons and approved premises such as bail hostels. They apply regardless of whether or not someone has the ability to make specific decisions for themselves at specific times. There may be times when an adult has care and support needs and is unable to protect themselves for a short, temporary period – for instance, when they are in hospital under anaesthetic.

If someone moves or is moved out of their local authority home area, their new local authority has the responsibility to respond to safeguarding concerns and to ensure any necessary enquiry is undertaken.

There is an increased focus in the Act in relation to safeguarding on carers, who may witness or report abuse, or be a victim or perpetrator (intentionally or unintentionally). The responsibility to safeguard carers is in line with the duty to assess carers.

Our understanding and recognition of the ways in which an adult may suffer significant harm are constantly expanding. They include:

- physical abuse;

- domestic violence and abuse;

- sexual abuse;

- psychological or emotional abuse;

- financial or material abuse;

- modern slavery;

- discriminatory abuse;

- organisational or institutional abuse;

- neglect or acts of omission;

- self-neglect or self-abuse.

It is important to be aware of the signs and indicators of each form of abuse and to record the category of abuse which is suspected or disclosed so that a pattern of incidents can be built up. It is also important to be aware of other potential causes of these signs and indicators to avoid identifying an incident or pattern of behaviour as abusive when it is not.

Activity 7.1

1. Does Carl (see pages 6–7) meet the three criteria necessary before a section 42 safeguarding enquiry can be considered?
2. What categories of abuse or neglect might arise in his case?
3. Is there anyone else you need to consider in terms of safeguarding?

Comment

Carl is an adult, with care and support needs. His physical disability, dependence and communication difficulties mean that he may be unable to protect himself from the risk of abuse, but this is not certain and would need to be assessed in the context of any specific risk. For instance, he might be quite able to resist and report an overt physical attack on the street, but unable to identify that his money is being misused. In addition to physical and financial abuse, Carl may be particularly vulnerable to psychological abuse, organisational abuse (in the short-stay setting), and neglect or self-neglect.

You might also need to consider any risk posed by Carl to other members of the family. It is reported that he has put his arm through a window; it would be important to explore whether this was accidental or deliberate, and whether he has acted violently on other occasions, to himself or others. Carers often have a very high tolerance of potentially harmful behaviour from those for whom they care and you may need to help Wendy to re-evaluate the level of risk involved. Finally, if Carl's young nephew is witnessing abuse between members of the household, this could lead to the involvement of children's services to protect him.

An enquiry is any action that is taken (or instigated) by a local authority, under section 42 of the Care Act 2014, in response to indications of abuse or neglect in relation to an adult with care and support needs who is at risk and is unable to protect themselves because of those needs. It may be preceded by an informal information-gathering process to find out if abuse may have taken place or is taking place. The local authority may decide that another organisation should carry out the enquiry, but it retains overall accountability and will need to agree and monitor timescales and follow-up actions. It might take the form of a conversation with the individual concerned and/or their representative or advocate. It might involve another organisation or individual, or a more formal process, perhaps leading to a formal multi-agency plan to ensure the well-being of the adult concerned. Many enquiries will need a great deal of input from a social care practitioner, often a social worker. Other professionals may have a role for some aspects, based on their expert knowledge or their involvement with the individual.

Whatever form the enquiry takes, recording of it must include:

- details of the safeguarding concern and who raised it;
- views and wishes of the adult affected, at the beginning and over time, and where appropriate the views of their family;
- any immediate action agreed with the adult or their representative;
- reasons for all actions and decisions;
- details of who else is consulted or the concern is discussed with;
- any timescales agreed for action;
- sign-off from a line manager and/or the local safeguarding lead or designated adult safeguarding manager.

A safeguarding enquiry may not necessarily result in a safeguarding response, such as an investigation by the police or the relevant health and social care regulator. It could lead to a new or revised care and support plan for the adult involved and/or their carer. It is important to note that an adult with care and support needs can be the person responsible for the abuse or neglect.

Non-statutory enquiries ('other safeguarding enquiries') may be carried out or instigated in response to concerns about carers, or about adults who do not have care and support needs but who may still be at risk of abuse or neglect and to whom the local authority has a well-being duty under section 1 of the Care Act 2014.

Denial of access

Denial of access in pursuit of a safeguarding enquiry may take the obvious form of denial of access to the premises altogether, by a family member, friend or other informal carer. It may be that a third party insists on being present, so that you cannot interview on their own the person who may be at risk of abuse or neglect. This is not necessarily a sign that something is amiss. They may distrust social workers or they may assume that the worker is there to remove the individual from their care. It will be important to respond to their concerns, while remaining honest about the purpose of the intervention. Finally, the person at the heart of the enquiry may insist that a third party remains present: in this case, if the individual has capacity to make this choice, the issue of access does not arise in terms of the law.

There is no automatic right of access for the local authority, or for social workers, for the purpose of safeguarding or any other enquiries. A court order needs to be used as a last resort because of the difficulty of maintaining an ongoing relationship once the courts are involved and for the very pragmatic reason that the courts will want to be assured that all alternatives have been explored before making an order. It may be possible, through negotiation, providing information and the use of your professional skills, to assuage the concerns which underpin the refusal of access. You may be able to arrange to speak to the person in another setting, perhaps at work or their day centre or respite facility. It may be possible to make use of other protective factors, such as family, friends, community groups or other professionals, to support the individual and to monitor the situation while you continue the conversation. Voluntary agencies may be seen in more positive light than statutory authorities.

In moving towards legal action to gain access, you need to consider whether the refusal of access is unreasonable and whether the circumstances justify intervention. The current and potential risks of intervening, as well as of not intervening, need to be taken into account and any action taken needs to be in proportion to these risks. These principles of necessity and proportionality link to the principle of choosing the least restrictive option in section 1 of the Mental Capacity Act, which requires that, in respect of an act or decision done for a person who lacks capacity, consideration must be given to achieving the person's best interests in a manner which is least restrictive of the person's rights and freedom of action. In its turn, this builds on the statutory *Code of Practice* for the Mental Health Act 1983:

> People taking action without a patient's consent must attempt to keep to a minimum the restrictions they impose on a patient's liberty, having regard to the purpose for which the restrictions are imposed.

> (Department of Health, 2008b, 1.3)

This is consistent with section 1 of the Care Act 2014, which states that a local authority exercising its functions under Part 1 of the Act in the case of an individual must promote that individual's well-being and have regard to a number of factors, including the need to ensure that any restrictions on the individual's rights or freedom of action are kept to the minimum necessary for achieving the purpose for which the function is being exercised.

Whatever decisions are taken (even – or especially – if it is decided to take no action) need clear and full recording, along with the reasons for them, and they should be shared as is necessary and useful. It is likely that you will want to seek advice from senior managers and your legal team, unless there is risk to life and limb that requires immediate intervention.

If the person has been assessed as lacking mental capacity in relation to a matter relating to their welfare, the Court of Protection has the power to make an order under section 16(2) of the Mental Capacity Act relating to a person's welfare, which makes the decision on that person's behalf to allow access to an adult lacking capacity. The court can also appoint a deputy to make welfare decisions for that person.

The Mental Health Act 1983, section 115, grants powers for an Approved Mental Health Professional (AMHP) to enter any premises (other than a hospital) of a person with a mental disorder if there is reasonable cause to believe that the person is not receiving adequate care, as long as the practitioner produces authenticated identification.

Section 135(1) of the Mental Health Act gives magistrates' courts the power, on application by an AMHP, to allow the police to enter premises using force if necessary and to remove a person to a place of safety if there is reasonable cause to suspect that they are suffering from a mental disorder and (a) have been, or are being, ill treated, neglected or not kept under proper control, or (b) are living alone and unable to care for themselves.

If there is an immediate and serious risk to a person or a property, the police can be asked to use their power to enter premises without a warrant under section 17(1) (e) of the Police and Criminal Evidence Act 1984. The police also have the power to enter premises and arrest a person for an indictable offence under section 17(1) (b) of the same Act.

Activity 7.2

Carl's mother is present at your first meeting with him and, because of the difficulties for you of communicating directly with him, answers for him much of the time. When she turns to Carl and says 'That's right, isn't it, lad?', Carl nods, but it is not clear how far he is following the conversation or is engaging with it. What practical steps can you take to try to ensure that you have an understanding of Carl's needs and wishes as he sees them?

Comment

Your initial visit to Carl is to reassess his needs following a change in eligibility criteria for services, not in response to safeguarding concerns. Given his level of dependence and your difficulty in understanding his speech, it is appropriate that someone who knows him well and who can interpret his speech for you is present. It will still be important to begin to build a relationship and to communicate directly with him, through pictures, simple yes/no questions or by sharing an activity he enjoys. An opportunity may arise for you to spend time with him on his own, perhaps in the garden or by asking to see his room. It is also possible to meet Carl in other settings and with others familiar with his speech, in his short-stay setting and to compare what he and they say and, importantly, his non-verbal communication.

Introducing Carl and his family to others in a similar situation may broaden their knowledge of the options open to Carl and also help to allay any fears his mother has about him living more independently.

Provisions for formal and informal advocacy with regard to assessment, safeguarding and mental capacity are considered further on in this chapter.

Self-determination and capacity in safeguarding adults

The Mental Capacity Act and the Care Act are intended to be complementary, not contradictory. Both aim to enable individuals to maintain their independence and to exercise as much control as possible over their lives, and any care and support they receive.

In adult safeguarding enquiries, the five principles of the Mental Capacity Act still apply:

- capacity is to be assumed, unless there is evidence otherwise;
- capacity needs to be maximised, by providing appropriate help and support (for instance, assistance to communicate or careful consideration of the best time of intervention);
- unwise or eccentric decisions do not in themselves prove lack of capacity;
- in making a decision for or about a person who lacks capacity, act in their best interests;
- the least restrictive option should be chosen.

Under the Care Act 2014 local authorities have a duty of advocacy which applies to adults who are the subject of a safeguarding enquiry or Safeguarding Adults Review if their care and support needs result in 'substantial difficulty' in being involved in decision making and no appropriate person is available to support them and to represent their views. Four areas need to be taken into account in deciding whether there is substantial difficulty:

1. Can the person understand the relevant information?

2. Can the person retain the information?

3. Can the person use or weigh up the information?

4. Can the person communicate their views, wishes and feelings?

An appropriate person can be a family member or friend but cannot be someone who is paid to give care or treatment to the individual. If no appropriate person is available, the local authority (or another agency on their behalf) should appoint an independent advocate. All agencies involved in safeguarding need to know how to obtain the services of an independent advocate. If a safeguarding enquiry is urgent, it can begin without an advocate in place, but one needs to be appointed as soon as possible. Their role is to support and represent the individual, and to help them to be involved in key processes and interactions with the local authority. They can also help people to get information and advice on being safe and to spot potential warning signs of abuse or neglect. Advocates must be fully independent and must not be employed by the local authority or by any organisation commissioned to carry out assessments, care and support plans or reviews for the local authority.

Many adults who qualify for advocacy under the Care Act will also qualify for advocacy under the Mental Capacity Act. Did you recognise the four areas of substantial difficulty above? They are the same in both Acts and the same person can provide advocacy under both Acts, which is often easier for the individual and for the agencies involved. In a safeguarding situation, an Independent Mental Capacity Advocate can be available even if a suitable family member or friend is also available. In this case, the IMCA's remit is not only to support and represent the individual but also to make sure that the Mental Capacity Act is being followed.

If someone's capacity to make decisions about their own welfare varies, perhaps because of dementia or alcohol or substance use, it may be possible to agree with them when they have capacity to make such an agreement the care and support they wish to receive when they lack such capacity.

An adult with capacity may decide to accept a situation that you perceive as potentially or actually abusive or neglectful and they are free to do so unless:

• other people are at risk;

• a child is involved;

• the alleged perpetrator has care and support needs and may also be at risk;

- a serious crime has been committed;

- staff are implicated;

- coercion is involved.

If the person is at risk of a significant, negative impact, you can discuss your options with colleagues, but any decision must be informed by the principles of choice, respect and dignity, and the requirement to help the person to achieve the outcomes they want. Reconciling these principles with the need to promote their well-being will call on all your ingenuity.

Even if someone has capacity, they may be under duress or coercion. The Mental Capacity Act will not usually apply, but the power of the High Court to hear any case not covered by other legislation (its inherent jurisdiction) can be invoked to gain access to assess an individual through an access order.

If someone with capacity is acting in a way that there is a risk only to their own safety or well-being and they are under no undue influence from anyone else, then you can decide not to intervene and not to share safeguarding information with other partners. However, this is not the end of your responsibility towards them. You need to make sure that they are aware of the risks and the potential impact on their safety and well-being, and encourage them to develop strategies to protect themselves – for instance, involvement with a user-led organisation or support group. You can offer support to weigh up risks and benefits of different options and should seek to reach agreement with them about the level of risk they are taking. They may be willing for you to arrange for them to have an advocate or peer supporter or support for them to build their confidence and self-esteem, if it appears relevant.

Whatever level of ongoing support the person accepts or refuses, you will need to record your reasons for not intervening or for not sharing information, including details of your assessment of the person's capacity and of your conversations with them about the potential risks posed by their chosen action. Make sure they understand where they can go if they want to seek help in the future and what they can do to protect themselves, including talking to other people they trust. Build in some way of reviewing the situation, even if this is only at the level of agreeing that you will make follow up contact at an agreed time, and seek to ensure that your relationship is such that they would be willing to contact you in the future.

It may also be possible to work with the person who is perpetrating the abuse or neglect to reduce the future risk.

Sharing information without consent

The Data Protection Act 1998 permits information to be shared in a situation of 'vital interest' where it is critical to prevent serious harm or distress or where someone's life is threatened. However, if the only person who would suffer if the information is not shared is the subject of that information, and they have mental capacity to make a decision about it, then sharing it may not be justified.

The Care Act 2014 requires safeguarding information about an individual to be shared, even if they exercise their capacity to refuse to consent to this, if:

- other people are at risk;

- a child is involved;

- the alleged perpetrator has care and support needs and may also be at risk;

- a serious crime has been committed;

- staff are implicated;

- coercion is involved.

If it is necessary to share information about an individual without their consent because other people's safety is potentially at risk, it is good practice to tell them this and to explain why, unless this would increase the risk of harm to them, or to someone else, including the worker. You need to explore with them your concerns and the object of sharing the information. They will need to know who will be given the information and to be reassured that it will not be shared with anyone who does not need to know. You may find it helpful to explain the potential benefits to them of sharing the information and the potential consequences of not sharing it.

Self-neglect and refusal of assessment

The statutory guidance relating to the Care Act 2014 makes it clear that self-neglect is a form of abuse or neglect, if the person concerned has care and support needs. However, although it may be raised as a safeguarding concern, it is usually more likely to be dealt with as an intervention under the parts of the Care Act dealing with assessment, planning, information, advice and prevention. Assessment of the person's capacity to make decisions about their own well-being and of the level of risk incurred will be crucial, not least in limiting the future liability of the local authority. If someone has this capacity, they have the right to make decisions that others may see as self-neglect. If they do not want any safeguarding action to be taken, it may be reasonable not to intervene further, as long as:

- no one else is at risk;

- vital interests are not compromised – that is, there is no immediate risk of death or major harm;

- all decisions are explained and recorded;

- other agencies have been informed and involved as necessary.

The legislation makes it clear that adult safeguarding responses should be guided by the adult themselves, to achieve the outcome they want to achieve. This will involve the use of a strengths-based approach, and existing networks and relationships. Even if they do not accept the worker's assessment of their situation, the individual may be willing to work out a plan for future support and follow-up which is acceptable to them.

Activity 7.3

What steps might you consider if Carl is not taking his epilepsy medication regularly?

Comment

If Carl is regularly admitted to hospital because he has a grand mal fit after not taking his medication, it may be that he needs much clearer guidance and support to advise him when to take it, perhaps through linking it to meal-times or providing a tablet organiser. He may need prompting and supervising to take his tablets. If he says that he does not want to take the tablets, it may be possible to provide his medication in a form that he does find acceptable.

It might be informative to consider his response in different settings and with different people, as well as looking at the form of the medication itself. The consequences of not taking his medication would need to be explored with him, including any limitations on activities he enjoys. If Carl is still adamant that he does not want to take his medication and it is judged that he has capacity to take this decision, then it cannot be given without his consent, unless his life is at immediate risk. This does not mean accepting his decision for all time. The medication should still be offered regularly and discussions should continue with Carl about his reluctance and its consequences.

Carl's reluctance to take a shower can be tackled by a similar process, trying to find a place or method or person that makes getting clean more acceptable to him. However, although it may limit his activities and relationships, not showering is less likely to reach life-threatening proportions and Carl may be protected from harm more by knowing that he has the right to say no and to be heard. Adults receiving care and support need to know that, if they speak out, they will gain more control over their environment. This is illustrated by the story of a support worker who succeeded, after six months, in teaching a woman with profound and multiple disabilities to sign 'biscuit'. The worker's jubilant tour of the building to share this achievement ended abruptly when her manager asked 'and did you give her a biscuit?' Offering and respecting choices in small, everyday matters is key to people developing the understanding that they have rights and choices in bigger decisions.

It may be that an individual with capacity refuses to take up the offer of an initial assessment of their care and support needs and, again, they have every right to do so. The Department of Health advises in its statutory guidance on the implementation of the Care Act 2014 that adult social care departments should record all the steps they have taken to complete an assessment of the things a person wants to achieve, and the care and support they need. Intervening successfully depends on practitioners taking time to gain a person's trust and build a relationship and to go at the pace of the individual.

If it proves impossible to carry out an assessment, or care and support services are refused, you need to show that you have made reasonable attempts to do so and that information and advice has been made available to the individual on accessing care and support, and on raising safeguarding concerns. Any decisions taken and the considerations leading to them should be recorded in the light of the person's wishes, and their particular circumstances and actions should be reasonable and proportionate.

Duty to promote the well-being of the wider population

A local authority has the general duty, in partnership with other agencies, to promote the well-being of the wider population in the community it serves. In its broadest implementation, this will involve the participation of a wide range of departments within the local authority apart from that concerned with adult social care. It will involve targeting information and advice on all aspects of promoting well-being, including keeping safe, to specific populations. With regard to safeguarding adults, the aim is to prevent abuse and neglect from occurring or reoccurring wherever possible. This includes working with adults who may be at risk to help them to identify potentially abusive situations and to understand how they can protect themselves. Guidance and information will need to be provided to people on their rights and choices, how they can recognise the warning signs of adult abuse and neglect, and where they can access help and support. Helping people to reduce their social isolation is a key element in this area and pilot schemes are currently being evaluated.

Local Safeguarding Adults Boards also have an important role in developing and supporting the implementation of preventative strategies. We will explore this more in the next chapter.

Becoming a social worker

The importance of the issues discussed in this chapter to all roles that involve social work with adults is confirmed by the prominence afforded to them in the 2015 *Knowledge and Skills Statement for Social workers in Adult Services:*

Social workers must be able to recognise the risk indicators of different forms of abuse and neglect and their impact on individuals, their families or their support networks and should prioritise the protection of children and adults in vulnerable situations whenever necessary. This includes working with those who self-neglect. Social workers who work with adults must take an outcomes-focused, person-centred approach to safeguarding practice, recognising that people are experts in their own lives and working alongside them to identify person-centred solutions to risk and harm.

(Department of Health, 2015, p3)

Chapter Summary

If a concern is raised that an adult is at risk of abuse or neglect, the local authority needs to ascertain if they have care and support needs and, if so, whether they are able to protect themselves from abuse and neglect. If an adult at risk of being abused or neglected cannot keep themselves safe from abuse or neglect because of their care and support needs, then the local authority's safeguarding duty applies. If they are able to protect themselves, despite having care and support needs, then a safeguarding response may not be appropriate.

This safeguarding duty applies regardless of the person's eligibility for local authority resources. Although someone with capacity to do so may decline assessment or intervention under this duty, the local authority must still do what it can to ensure the person's well-being.

Further Reading

Braye, S, Orr, D and Preston-Shoot, M (2015) Learning lessons about self-neglect? An analysis of serious case reviews, *Journal of Adult Protection*, 17(1): 3–18 provides a useful overview of the findings and recommendations of serious case reviews in cases involving self-neglect.

Mantell, A and Scragg, T (2011) *Safeguarding Adults in Social Work*. Exeter: Learning Matters. This book in this series preceded the Care Act 2014, but the sections on the development of effective professional and interprofessional practice with adults at risk extend what is possible in a single chapter here.

Social Care Institute for Excellence (SCIE) has extensive and up-to-date resources on safeguarding policy and practice, available at: www.scie.org.uk/adults/safeguarding/resources/

Chapter 8

Personalisation and partnership working

Meeting professional standards

This chapter will help you to develop the following selected capabilities, to the appropriate level, from the social work Professional Capabilities Framework.

Professionalism

- Be able to explain the role of the social worker in a range of contexts, and uphold the reputation of the profession.

Values and ethics

- Demonstrate respectful partnership work with service users and carers, eliciting and respecting their needs and views, and promoting their participation within decision making wherever possible.

Rights and justice

- Address oppression and discrimination applying the law to protect and advance people's rights, recognising how legislation can constrain or advance these rights.

Intervention and skills

- Use appropriate assessment frameworks, applying information gathering skills to make and contribute to assessments, whilst continuing to build relationships and offer support. Share information consistently in ways that meet legal, ethical and agency requirements.

The Care Act 2014 requires local authorities to carry out their care and support responsibilities in a way that promotes integration with a wide range of partners, including health, housing and leisure services. In particular, they are required to put into place joint health and well-being strategies and to promote joint case work.

Partners must co-operate with each other when asked to do so, unless what is asked is incompatible with their own functions or duties.

The College of Social Work, in its 'Real Social Work' campaign announced at its annual conference in March 2015, set as one of its five priorities for government for 2015 and beyond 'to put social work at the heart of integrated care for adults'.

The personalisation agenda remains central to adult social care and its extension to health provision is in line with this focus on integration of provision for adults. Its promotion of universal services fits well with the Care Act's well-being agenda and its promotion of person-centred care and support planning is fulfilled in the Act's expectation that adults will be responsible for assessing their own needs, and designing their own care and support plans to meet these needs. The local authority remains responsible for assessing eligibility for local authority resourcing through personal budgets and for accounting for money used in this way.

All of this has particular implications for arrangements for sharing information and for meeting care and support needs when working with someone who lacks capacity, and it is these issues which concern us in this chapter.

Self-assessment of care and support needs, and self-direction of the plan for care and support, is now the default position in the assessment of adults and this means that the processes involved must be as accessible as possible, not least in terms of language, literacy and digital inclusion. In determining in rare cases that it is inappropriate for an individual to assess or plan to meet their own needs, the practitioner will need to consider their capacity to do so, alongside their capabilities and personal strengths. They may be able to take on these tasks if their communication needs are met or if they are provided with other support. The practitioner has a duty to promote independent advocacy to help involve the adult and their carer in assessing their needs and planning for their care if they face significant difficulty in doing so. In all cases, the local authority retains its duty of care and the practitioner remains responsible for ensuring that the assessment is complete and accurate. This accountability is not to restrict choice or stifle innovation.

Activity 8.1

1. In the case set in the community (see pages 6–7), who is your client?
2. What might make it difficult to maintain this understanding?
3. Who will you seek to involve in the assessment?

Comment

Carl is clearly the primary client, and I hope that you included him in your list of those who would need to be involved in his reassessment, along with his immediate family. However, focus may move from Carl because of his communication difficulties and because of the needs of his mother for care and support, which enables her to work, and the family doctor's emphasis on her practical and emotional needs as paramount in sustaining the situation. There may be hospital as well as primary healthcare short-stay staff to consult. The personal assistant will also have relevant information to offer. The college and school contacts are now some time ago, but there may be key contextual and historical information on file from these settings. It may be appropriate to access local housing providers, carers' groups and user-led groups to begin to scope what the options are for Carl. Finally, it is important to ask whether anyone is exercising either type of Lasting Power of Attorney for Carl. It would be frustrating for all concerned to get to the end of the reassessment only to discover that his absent father has the legal right to make decisions regarding Carl's welfare.

If no eligible needs are identified and it is decided not to meet non-eligible needs, a written explanation of this decision should be provided. For care and support needs to be met by the local authority, a sufficient personal budget needs to be agreed and recorded in the plan, with as much flexibility allowed as possible in its use. It is expected that practitioners will explain to people their right to direct payments, without insisting that they receive their personal budgets in this form. Provision of direct payments is to be reviewed within six months and then every 12 months but without placing a disproportionate reporting burden on the individual. If provision through direct payments is ended, it is important to ensure that there is no gap in provision.

If someone lacks the capacity to ask for a direct payment, the request must be made by someone who is authorised under the Mental Capacity Act 2005 to make decisions about the adult's care and support or a person nominated by a person so authorised or a person considered suitable by the local authority. In this situation, the local authority must make direct payments if it is satisfied that the person making the request will act in the adult's best interests in arranging the care and support to be funded by the direct payment, that they are capable of doing so (with any help available to them) and that making a direct payment is appropriate to meet the person's needs.

Those with multiple and complex needs may be likely to benefit most from the creative and flexible use of their personal budgets, but they and their families may also have the least ability or energy to manage them. Practitioners can help by ensuring that personal budgets take full account of all costs, including recruitment, selection and training of new workers, payroll services and employer's liabilities such as National Insurance payments, holiday and sick pay and pension contributions. Personal assistants can be employed without a Disclosure and Barring Service check, but this is an obvious way of reducing the risk of abuse and is much more likely to take place if the cost is included in the personal budget.

This is only one element of the safeguards that need to be put in place to ensure that the shift to self-assessment and personal budgets does not increase the risk of abuse or neglect. More independence may mean exposure to more risk.

Activity 8.2

Carl's support worker is concerned that he is being exploited by people he meets in the pub and sees as his friends, but who constantly persuade him that it is his round without reciprocating. Carl is adamant that he is happy with the situation and doesn't want these concerns sharing with anyone else, in case his freedom is further restricted. What can be done?

Comment

Since he has capacity and no one else is at risk and no serious crime has been committed, Carl's decision not to have this safeguarding concern shared has to be respected. Nevertheless, the support worker can discuss with him ways in which the risks can be reduced – perhaps by taking less money to the pub?

Nevertheless, the aim of assessment and care planning needs to be risk appraisal, not risk avoidance, with a proportionate tolerance of acceptable risks, in the context of an individual's wishes, lifestyle and background, and their quality of life and dignity. It is also worth bearing in mind that over-protection and lack of opportunities to develop coping skills may actually put adults at more risk.

The environment in which care and support is provided will provide particular considerations for the practitioner.

Family home

A parent's legal right to make decisions on behalf of their child ends abruptly at 18, even if they are living in the same household. However, this may not be apparent to the adult child and things may continue much as they have done. The interaction of finances can have a huge impact on the discussions about how care and support are provided for someone of any age, especially if the individual's benefits form an important element of the household income or family members are employed as carers. For a carer in employment, the provision of appropriately timed care and support may be essential for them to be able to continue in employment. In this context, it can be difficult to maintain focus on the person who is in need of care and support, especially if there are communication difficulties or a family member is acting as their advocate, formally or informally.

When care and support are provided by family members or other unpaid carers, it is not governed by any regulations, standards or inspection body. It is difficult when care is less than ideal to know whether it is necessary to intervene or whether this will do more harm than good. The discussion in the previous chapter about the interaction of risk and capacity assessment with your safeguarding duty is relevant here, but it is likely to be complicated by the individual's fear of damaging a valued relationship or of betraying someone they love. Their wishes and feelings are important, but so, too, is the level of risk.

It may be that medication is not being given exactly as prescribed, that the hoist provided after a moving and handling assessment is kept in the garage 'out of the way' or that money is not being used for its allocated purpose. It is important to assess whether the person with care and support needs is at direct risk of significant harm as a result. For instance, failure to help them to change position may be resulting in pressure sores, or the diversion of money may leave them hungry or cold.

In extreme cases, where an adult lacks capacity, informal carers can be prosecuted under section 44 of the Mental Capacity Act 2005 for wilful neglect. More commonly, and especially if the abuse or neglect is the result of carer stress, you may need to address both people's needs at once. It may even provide leverage to argue for additional resources for the carer.

It is worth noting that an adult with care and support needs may be responsible for harming someone else in the household, including their carer, and that the mandate for a safeguarding enquiry requires only that someone is in need of care and support, and not necessarily in receipt of it.

When an individual is employing their own personal assistants, it can be particularly hard to identify and tackle poor care, and whoever arranges the care and support package (usually the local authority) should satisfy itself that a person with care and support needs knows who to contact if they are dissatisfied with the support they are getting.

Domestic abuse

'Domestic violence and abuse' (Home Office, 2013) defines domestic abuse as:
Any incident or pattern of incidents of controlling, coercive or threatening behaviour, violence or abuse between those aged 16 or over, who are or have been intimate partners or family members regardless of gender or sexuality. This definition includes (but is not limited to) physical violence or psychological, sexual, financial and emotional abuse. It is interesting for our purposes in two respects. First, it broadens the range of individuals and relationships in which domestic abuse may occur well beyond the general perception of an adult male abusing an adult female with whom he lives and has a sexual relationship. In particular, it can apply to members of the same family, where one is the other's carer or where a more complex and evolving reciprocal pattern of care is in place. Second, it refers to coercive behaviour, and we have seen how this may allow intervention on safeguarding grounds where it is stated by the potential victim that they do not want any action to be taken, even if they have capacity.

If the abuser is the person's carer, they will have considerable power and control over the victim, who may be reliant on them and unable to see any way out; this may be particularly true for someone with a mental disorder. The CAADA-DASH risk assessment checklist enables a practitioner to assess the level of risk in a format which is accepted by police forces and many other partner agencies. It was developed by the Association of Chief Police Officers in partnership with Co-ordinated Action Against Domestic Abuse (now SafeLives): DASH stands for domestic abuse, stalking and 'honour'-based violence (checked on its website).

For a safeguarding enquiry to be initiated, the usual three criteria must be met: that someone has care and support needs; that they are experiencing or at risk of abuse or neglect; and that they are not able to protect themselves because of their care and support needs.

Whichever route is taken, the following principles apply:

- seek to develop a good relationship with the adult at risk and put their views and wishes at the forefront of all discussions;

- be alert to patterns of coercive or controlling behaviour and be aware that an adult at risk may refuse to report abuse because of fear;

- consider any additional likely impact of abuse on an adult with care and support needs;

- understand how local safeguarding services and MARACs (Multi-Agency Risk Assessment Conferences) fit together;

- be aware of the legislative options and local resources that are available both to safeguarding teams and to MARACs, so that practitioners know the full range of responses available to them when supporting an adult with care and support needs.

Making Safeguarding Personal 2015

The Making Safeguarding Personal programme 2015 is led by the Association of Directors of Adult Social Services and the Local Government Association, and funded by the Department of Health to encourage individuals, families, carers and agencies to work together to keep people safe and to support their choices. It arose partly from the Department of Health consultation exercise in 2009 on *No Secrets*, which demonstrated that in this area, as in others, people wanted to have control of the issues affecting them and that their experience of the safeguarding process was as important as its outcome.

In order to measure the success of the process, its desired outcome needs to be defined, and Making Safeguarding Personal asks for a much greater involvement of the individual (or their best interests decision maker, representative or advocate, if they lack capacity) and their wishes and preferences in this decision making. It suggests that three levels of action are needed to make sure that safeguarding processes do what the individuals concerned want.

1. Individuals need to be asked what their desired outcome is and this should be used as the basis of review, with both recorded for use by Safeguarding Adults Boards. There is an important recognition that desired outcomes may change over time.

2. Boards should act to improve outcomes.

3. Universities or other research organisations can be involved to evaluate more formally areas such as service delivery, staff development and information systems.

This requires a shift in practice from carrying out a step-by-step process to working alongside the individual concerned to improve their outcomes, as they define them and as they change along the way. It has very clear practice implications, in terms of asking what people want and recording this, but being honest with them when this is impossible, because of resource implications or your assessment of their capacity, without any coercion being exercised. It will involve you in helping people to make choices and in supporting them to manage risks, although not necessarily with intervention from social services: relatives, housing or health services could have a key role. If a safeguarding plan is needed to keep an adult safe, they – or their advocate or representative – should contribute to this and agree to it. At the review stage, it will be good practice to ask the person's view of the extent to which their desired outcome has been met.

Health funding for care and support needs

For most people, their care and support needs will be met from the local authority adult social care budget, with a financial assessment to decide what proportion of the cost should be met by the individual concerned. However, in some very specific cases, the person acquires the right to health funding of their care and support needs, which is therefore provided with no cost to them and no need for a financial assessment.

Section 117 of the Mental Health Act 1983 establishes the right to free mental health aftercare on discharge from hospital for someone who has been compulsorily detained in hospital under section 3 of the Act, or for someone who was in a psychiatric hospital because they were detained there by the sentence of a criminal court or for someone transferred to a psychiatric hospital from prison. It does not apply to people who have been detained in hospital for assessment under section 2 of the Mental Health Act or to anyone detained in an emergency under section 4 of the Act. It will not usually apply to voluntary patients in a psychiatric hospital, unless they became a voluntary patient after previously being compulsorily detained under section 3.

For those to whom it applies, section 117 means that they will not need to have a financial assessment for social or health services arising from or related to their mental disorder. Reassessment is required before section 117 services are withdrawn.

Section 75 of the Care Act 2014 for the first time defines 'after care services' as those which:

1. meet a need arising from or related to the person's mental disorder and

2. reduce the risk of a deterioration of the person's mental condition.

It also amends the definition of the local authority or NHS Trust responsible from that where the discharged person is resident, to that where they were ordinarily resident immediately before their admission. Section 75(6) allows a local authority to be required to comply with an individual's preference for accommodation provided under section 117, even if it costs more than the authority's usual cost and for the individual to top up this amount, and the local authority's contribution can be by direct payments. As a result, mental health teams within hospitals will find themselves supporting individuals to manage direct payments and personal budgets set up on discharge.

If services are provided for someone with a mental disorder by a range of providers, the individual is assessed under the Care Programme Approach and a care co-coordinator is appointed. This is likely to be the case for those meeting the criteria for free aftercare under section 117, but may also be provided for someone who was a voluntary patient but who is discharged with complex needs.

NHS continuing healthcare is provided and funded solely by the NHS for individuals who are not in hospital and who have been assessed as having a 'primary health need'. Unlike social and community care services, it is free regardless of who provides the care or where it is provided. If an initial screening suggests that someone may be eligible for continuing healthcare, the Clinical Commissioning Group is responsible for ensuring that a full assessment is carried out by a multidisciplinary team of at least two health or care professionals already involved in the person's care. Using the Decision Support Tool, they will assess whether the main or primary care needs relate to the person's health in a range of areas:

- behaviour;
- cognition;
- communication;
- psychological/emotional needs;
- mobility;
- nutrition;
- continence;
- skin;
- breathing;
- symptom control through medication;
- altered states of consciousness;
- other significant needs.

If so, these needs are met from health funding, with no charge to the individual concerned.

Activity 8.3

Is Carl likely to have access to any health funding if he lives in his own flat?

Comment

There is no evidence that Carl has ever been compulsorily defined under the Mental Health Act, so he will not be entitled to funding under section 117. It is also unlikely that he will meet the criteria for continuing healthcare, unless it can be argued that he needs regular treatment that only someone under the supervision of a qualified nurse can give (for instance, rectal valium). Carl is in receipt of health-funded short stays, while his mother is his main carer. If this is provided purely as respite for his family carers, it will no longer be required if a fully independent care package is set up. However, the NHS Trust may be willing to maintain some input to Carl's package, given his health needs.

Until very recently, someone in receipt of a personal budget to fund the care and support needs they had agreed with their local authority was faced with a difficult choice if they became eligible for their care and support needs to be met through health funding. This would cost them nothing, but might mean that they had to relinquish the care plan they had established using their personal budget, typically through personal assistants employed by them in their own home and community, and accept a health-resourced package which might require them to be in a certain place to require care, perhaps at home for a long period of time for a district nurse visit, or at a day centre or even resident on a ward. Personal health budgets have been piloted in a number of places and, since October 2014, adults receiving continuing healthcare have had a right to have a personal health budget. This can be used flexibly and alongside a personal budget (which can be paid into the same account) to pay for a wide range of items, including therapies, personal care and equipment. The care plan to spend the budget is drawn up by the individual with their health team and the funding can be provided as direct payments. People do not have to receive their health funding through a personal health budget, but their use is likely to extend, with local NHS organisations free to offer personal health budgets to people who may benefit. It is worth noting that the future provision of personal health budgets will also make it possible for many older people to remain in their own homes, when historically they were forced into residential or nursing care (leading to DOLS authorisations), because traditional health service provision in the community could not meet their needs.

Paid carers and organisational abuse

The first annual safeguarding return, a record of investigations collected from all the councils in England for the year to March 2014, was published by the government's Health and Social Care Information Centre (HSCIC) on 14 October 2014. In 40 per cent of substantiated allegations, the source of the risk was social care support or a paid, contracted or commissioned service. A total of 28 per cent of concluded referrals involved adults who were found to lack capacity; in a further 29 per cent of concluded referrals, the capacity of the adult at risk was unknown.

Local authorities have a duty to make sure that the care and support they commission are provided safely and to a high standard, while also recognising and tackling the abuse and neglect that happens in community and domestic settings.

If abuse or neglect takes place in a service such as a care home, home care agency, day centre, hospital or college, the employer has first responsibility as the provider of the service. They need to inform the local authority (and the local Clinical Commissioning Group if the NHS is the commissioner). The well-being of the person concerned is of paramount importance and the employer needs to take action to protect the adult concerned from further harm, by removing the staff or volunteers involved or perhaps by providing training and supervision. The employer also carries out the initial investigation, unless there is a serious conflict of interest or reason to suppose that it will not be tackled effectively or it is possible that a criminal offence has been committed. As we have seen, the Deprivation of Liberty Safeguards can be applied only in registered care homes and hospitals and not in supported living or sheltered housing or in someone's own home. If safeguards are in place for the individual concerned, the supervisory body will need to be informed and involved in all subsequent actions.

Multi-agency procedures must reflect statutory guidance and spell out for local care providers the circumstances when the police must be involved, or when to inform the local authority, Clinical Commissioning Group or Care Quality Commission and what their role will be. If domiciliary or residential care is provided by a private agency, Care Quality Commission registration may be involved. The police will have an interest if criminal activity is alleged – for instance, theft. It will be important to ascertain if anyone else is at risk from the same carer.

There may be occasions when the local authority is notified in its role as commissioner, without the adult safeguarding team being involved. The Care Quality Commission needs to satisfy itself that a provider registered with it is competent to address the issue quickly and effectively.

Many of the issues that are raised as safeguarding concerns (such as falls, pressure sores, medication errors and inadequate nutritional provision) may not be malicious but are, rather, examples of poor quality care. Practitioners need to differentiate between the two to avoid making safeguarding enquiries unnecessarily, so that police and adult safeguarding teams focus on potential criminal acts and malicious behaviour rather than poor care practices. However, some past cases of abuse were first thought to be poor care. Local multi-agency policies and procedures should make it clear when it is necessary to refer concerns about an adult at risk to local safeguarding channels and you will need to exercise your professional judgement in this, supported by your manager.

Examples of poor care are a one-off medication error (even though this could have very serious consequences), an incident of under-staffing, resulting in a person's incontinence pad being unchanged all day, poor quality, unappetising food or one missed visit by a care worker from a care home.

Potential causes for concern that standards of care are so poor that adults are put at increased risk and that organisational abuse may be taking place include a series of medication errors, an increase in the number of visits from a care home to the Accident and Emergency Department (especially if the same injuries happen more than once), nutritionally inadequate food, signs of neglect such as clothes being dirty, repeated missed visits by a home care agency, an increase in the number of complaints received about the service or in the use of agency or bank staff and a pattern of missed GP or dental appointments. Lack of flexibility and choice for adults using the service, and failure to make sure residents have privacy and personal dignity, are harder to measure.

It is clear that unless good recording systems are in place to reveal a pattern of incidents such as these, they are likely to be picked up only by external, independent inspection and monitoring. Interestingly, an unusually low number of safeguarding concerns as well as a high number may indicate organisational abuse, with collusion at all levels to hide this. Similarly, high staff turnover or no staff turnover may both indicate problems. It is good practice to keep the commissioner of the service and the Care Quality Commission fully informed of the action being taken if single instances of poor or neglectful care are repeated, patterns of harm are identified and other people are put at risk. The Safeguarding Adults Board needs to be made aware of any such concerns in its area and of the actions taken to remedy the situation.

Repeated instances of neglect or poor practice may indicate organisational abuse, if standards of care are so poor that residents are put at risk and the organisation fails to address problems that are brought to its attention. Each local authority and regulator involved should be notified and each individual affected should be consulted about where they want to live, regardless of whether the care setting is to close. It may be that the risks of an unplanned move outweigh the risks of staying. The Care Act 2014 places a duty on the local authority to promote the care and support market and to meet people's needs if care fails.

Once the local authority is informed, it has a duty to find out what has happened and to decide if further action is needed. If the provider is not responding adequately, the local authority may need to carry out its own enquiry and to monitor the follow-up action. It may advise the provider that the Care Quality Commission, Disclosure and Barring Service or relevant professional regulator is informed. It will definitely need to ensure that all actions and decisions are clearly recorded and can require information to be passed to the local Safeguarding Adults Board as well as to the local commissioners.

If concerns are raised about the standard of care received in a hospital or in health service commissioned care, the local NHS Trust or Clinical Commissioning Group can ask a clinician to establish if this has resulted from poor practice, intentional abuse or avoidable neglect. It may be concluded that the service provider can resolve the issue or that external clinical or regulatory enforcement action is needed. This will usually be more appropriate than a local authority- or social worker-led enquiry under section 42 of the Care Act 2014.

However, reliance on clinical governance systems could place long-stay residents in services provided, or commissioned, by health Trusts at greater risk of unchallenged abuse, particularly where it is widespread and condoned by qualified staff, as happened at Winterbourne View.

Partly in response to the serious case review into Winterbourne View, the Care Act 2014 makes the NHS and, specifically, the local Clinical Commissioning Group one of the three statutory core partners of the Safeguarding Adults Board. Many boards will also invite local NHS Provider Trusts and General Practitioner representatives to sit on the board. The Act also requires the NHS and local authority to come to an agreement about what constitutes a 'serious incident', what is a safeguarding concern and what are appropriate responses to each. Statistics and details of incidents affecting patient safety are to be reported to, and by, the board.

In addition, Part 2 of the Act places a duty of candour about failings in their care on providers of healthcare and adult social services registered with the Care Quality Commission. This requires them to ensure transparency and honesty when things go wrong, to apologise to the person concerned as soon as possible, and to provide them with support and continuing information.

Other agencies

Independent, voluntary and user-led organisations are likely to take the lead in providing advocacy and preventative services, in offering a voice to those with care and support needs and their carers, and in getting out information about potential risks.

Housing providers have a key role to play, especially if no other services are in place, within and outside Supporting People regulations, which build in safeguarding standards. Some serious case reviews in the past have concluded that housing providers could play a more effective role in safeguarding. They will need encouragement to work with social care if someone is not eligible for social care services, or refuses them or is neglecting themselves. Housing providers may get involved in training their staff (especially around the right to report potential abuse without consent), in liaison, in training for the care and support needs of individuals, and in making support available for carers and for people who behave in an anti-social way. Where housing providers are offering support and monitoring contracts for tenants with care and support needs, boundary issues may arise and need to be resolved. They may need to ensure that they have adequate IT systems to store sensitive data and profiling. Safeguarding Adults Boards may want to have housing represented on the board, not as a statutory partner, but to draw on their input, collaboration and advice. However, there will be many housing providers in their area. One solution is to form a housing forum or subgroup which then reports to and from the board. Relationships between housing and social care providers may not always be amicable, with housing providers complaining that thresholds for safeguarding referrals are too high and social care teams claiming that housing providers fail to carry out risk and capacity assessments when these are necessary. Offering to train housing staff on the Mental Capacity Act and doing joint visits and assessments where there are issues of both social care and housing may help.

The Probation Service has responsibility for Multi-Agency Public Protection Arrangements (MAPPA) and a remit to work with victims of serious sexual and other violent crimes. It can also identify and help offenders at risk of abuse. Its aim is to reduce reoffending and thus protect the public and previous victims from serious harm.

Prison governors can attend Safeguarding Adults Boards by invitation, but the Care Act 2014 section 42 duty to make enquiries and section 44 duty to carry out Safeguarding Adults Reviews do not apply in prisons or in approved premises. However, statutory guidance to the Care Act requires local authorities to share information about people with care and support needs in or on their way to or from prison or other custodial settings, including the sharing of information about risk to the prisoner and others where this is relevant. Safeguarding Adults Boards are expected to have a framework and process for any affiliated organisation to respond to allegations and issues of concern about a potential abuser.

The police can keep records on targets of abuse and on those who may pose a risk to others, and can share this information with their safeguarding partners for the purposes of protection. Their IT systems can help to identify repeat and vulnerable victims of anti-social behaviour.

The Fire and Rescue Service can support other agencies to recognise, assess and manage fire risks, and can provide safety advice and smoke alarms. Its officers can be well placed to identify neglect or abuse which is placing an adult at risk.

Criminal offences specific to people with mental disorder or lacking capacity

While the focus of the safeguarding provisions of the Care Act is learning, not blame, other legislation makes clear the criminality of specific types of abuse when the person abused has a mental disorder or lacks capacity.

The Sexual Offences Act 2003 prohibits any sexual activity between a care worker and a person with a mental disorder while the relationship of care continues. It applies whether the worker is paid or unpaid, whether or not the mentally disordered person has the capacity to consent, and whether or not the relationship is, in fact, consensual.

Section 127 of the Mental Health Act makes it an offence for staff in a hospital or mental nursing home to ill-treat or to wilfully neglect a person with a mental disorder. Ill-treatment needs to be deliberate, in that the person carrying it out understands that it is reckless or inexcusable ill-treatment, but it need not cause harm. Wilful neglect is defined as the failure to act. This has particular implications for staff who are aware that abuse is taking place but who do not report it. We shall look at whistleblowing and the legal protection available to whistleblowers later in this chapter.

The Mental Capacity Act 2005 (section 44) makes wilful neglect or mistreatment of an adult who lacks capacity a criminal offence.

Section 59 of the Safeguarding Vulnerable Groups Act 2006 established the Independent Safeguarding Authority to register workers and volunteers with vulnerable people and to keep a list of those barred from such work. If someone is dismissed or removed from their role because they are thought to have caused harm or to be a potential risk to children or to adults with care and support needs, those dismissing or removing them are required to report them to the ISA to be placed on its list of those barred from employment or volunteering in regulated activity. This is defined as paid or unpaid work involving regular or close contact with children; providing healthcare, personal care or funding for advertisements; or work involving making welfare decisions on behalf of those who lack capacity. The person to be barred does not have to be convicted of a crime. The Independent Safeguarding Authority and the Criminal Records Bureau merged to become the Disclosure and Barring Service on 1 December 2012. The Protection of Freedoms Bill amends its role, retaining the barring function, but abolishing registration monitoring and the category of controlled activity.

Information sharing and Safeguarding Adults Boards

Adult serious case reviews have long highlighted the need for all parties to communicate well and work jointly. We noted earlier how the failure of the local authority, health and housing services, the police and care providers to do so led to the death of Steven Hoskin.

The Care Act 2014 places a duty on local authorities to set up a Safeguarding Adults Board with core membership drawn from the local authority, the police and the National Health Service (specifically, the local Clinical Commissioning Group/s). Adult services departments should take the lead co-ordinating role in safeguarding adults who may be at risk, while the police lead on criminal investigations. The local chief of police is a statutory core member of the Safeguarding Adults Board and any criminal investigation takes precedence, because of the need to preserve and gather evidence.

If there is a reasonable suspicion that a crime may have been committed and the harm caused to the adult concerned was deliberate, malicious or reckless, then it is sensible to have a discussion with the lead officer in the local police force. In an emergency, if there are concerns that an adult is at immediate risk of serious harm, the police have the power to intervene if a person needs immediate assistance due to a health condition, injury or other life-threatening situation.

Otherwise, you will need to take into account the views and wishes of the adult at risk and the exact circumstances surrounding each individual case of suspected abuse or neglect. They may not want the police involved, perhaps because of complex family dynamics or personal relationships, but there may be risk of harm to another person. Local policies and procedures should be followed to ensure that information is shared appropriately. There may be situations that are technically a crime but where it is appropriate to consider what type of intervention will lead to the desired outcomes. The principle of proportionality applies here: to take the least intrusive and most appropriate action in proportion to the seriousness of the situation. If the crime is stealing a few pounds from a fellow resident, a minor physical altercation in sheltered housing or an overstretched carer hitting back, an informal discussion with the police together with the adult affected or their representative may be the best way to decide if police involvement is appropriate.

If there is any possibility that a criminal prosecution will be brought, the police need to be involved at the earliest opportunity to protect forensic evidence, both physical and verbal. Early contact with police may help to obtain vital evidence and witness statements, leading to a successful prosecution. Once police are involved, enquiries take precedence over others in progress and interaction with matters such as internal disciplinary hearings will need to be co-ordinated locally. A higher standard of proof is needed in criminal cases than in disciplinary or regulatory proceedings.

The Care Act explicitly recognises that safeguarding is everyone's concern, so it grants the power to include other relevant bodies on the board, in addition to the three core members. These may include local authority departments in addition to adult social care, fire and rescue services, prison and probation, housing, voluntary and independent organisations, advocacy groups, coroners, faith communities, and representatives from the Care Quality Commission, Crown Prosecution Service, Disclosure and Barring Service and the Office of the Public Guardian.

The Safeguarding Adults Board is required to produce an annual strategic plan for each financial year, stating how it plans to meet its main objectives and what each of its members will do to achieve them. It also needs to publish an annual report reviewing its plan, and the findings of safeguarding adults reviews (previously Serious Case Reviews) and the actions taken as a result.

One of the key purposes of the Safeguarding Adults Board is to permit and facilitate the sharing of relevant information between these partners, each of whom will have a Designated Adult Safeguarding Manager. This is in the context of complex networks and health, police and local authorities with different geographical boundaries. It will be necessary to develop a common language, with terms and definitions which mean the same to all those who need to use them, and shared and agreed perceptions of risk levels. There is also a need for joint approaches to those ineligible for social care support and to those who refuse support or who are at risk of significant harm because of self-neglect.

The Safeguarding Adults Board is likely to have a number of subgroups to provide and disseminate information. Forums are likely to include those with care and support needs, carers, providers of housing and other services, and regulators. It may be necessary to enable members of these groups to gain the skills and equipment to contribute to common databases which might help to identify people who are at risk of abuse.

The board will also need to ensure that it has good links with external organisations, including partnerships with neighbouring local authorities, child safeguarding and health and well-being boards, community safety partnerships and Multi-Agency Public Protection Arrangements (MAPPA), and Risk Assessment Conferences (MARACs). Co-location in multi-agency hubs can support this process, alongside virtual links and data sharing. Service commissioners may want to include an obligation to share information with partner organisations in the contracts they set up.

Accident and Emergency Departments and fire and rescue and ambulance services can function as early warning systems about possible safeguarding concerns. So, too, can complaints systems: it may be appropriate to treat a complaint as a safeguarding concern and to respond accordingly.

In line with the duty to permit and facilitate the sharing of information, the board's annual strategic plan will record the communication channels and protocols in place. The local authority, as lead safeguarding agency, should make sure that all partner organisations (not just the three statutory partners) have signed up to a local information-sharing protocol, which makes clear the channels and procedures for sharing information, including the information that needs to be shared, agreements about data security, retention and deletion, and what to tell people about information sharing and how. All partners need to ensure that their staff members understand the protocol and that they apply it. Frontline staff and volunteers should always report safeguarding concerns in line with their organisation's policy, usually to their line manager unless it is an emergency or there is a potential conflict of interest. The protocol will inform the sharing of information between partners.

The protocol is likely to include the following mandates for information sharing between partners:

- to prevent death or serious harm;
- to co-ordinate responses;
- to enable early intervention in order to prevent increasing risk;
- to develop preventative practice;
- to share good practice;
- to identify patterns of abuse and to identify others at risk;
- to help people to access support;
- to identify people who may pose a risk to others and so reduce risk;
- in the public interest (for instance, to prevent serious crime).

Emergency or life-threatening situations may warrant the sharing of information with relevant emergency services without consent. There may also be occasions when it is appropriate to contact the police or local authority for advice without giving any personal details of those concerned.

If there is continued reluctance from one partner to share information on a safeguarding concern, or in instances where an alerting organisation thinks that the local authority response is not sufficient, then the matter can be referred to the Safeguarding Adults Board for a decision. The board can also consider requests for the 'supply of information' under Clause 45 of the Care Act 2014, which covers the responsibilities of others to comply with requests for information from the Safeguarding Adults Board. An organisation can only refuse to comply if to do so would be incompatible with their own duties or have an adverse effect on the exercise of their functions.

Whistleblowing policies and practice

Standards across a range of professions require practitioners to report practices and situations which put at risk those for whom they care. The Health & Care Professions Council, which registers social workers and nurses among others, sets standards of conduct, performance and ethics which expect that practitioners must act in the best interests of service users and must protect service users from danger and has the following standards of proficiency for social workers:

- understand the need to protect, safeguard and promote the well-being of children, young people and vulnerable adults;

- be able to recognise and respond appropriately to situations where it is necessary to share info to safeguard service users and carers or others.

The *Code of Ethics* (2012) of the British Association of Social Workers states that *Social workers should be prepared to report bad practice using all available channels including complaints procedures and if necessary use public interest disclosure legislation and whistleblowing guidelines* (section 3.9).

Care workers and support workers are not subject to registration, but similar expectations are placed on them by voluntary codes and training requirements. The Skills for Care *Code of Conduct for Healthcare Support Workers and Adult Social Care Workers in England* (2013a) states that:

> *as a healthcare support worker or adult social care worker in England you must report any actions or omissions by yourself or colleagues that you feel may compromise the safety or care of people who use health and care services and, if necessary, use whistleblowing procedures to report any suspected wrongdoing.*

(p4)

National Minimum Training Standards (Skills for Care, 2013b) for these same groups require workers to know how and when to escalate any concerns, including the use of workplace policies:

> *you must report things that you feel are not right, are illegal or if anyone at work is neglecting their duties. This includes when someone's health and safety is in danger; danger to the environment; a criminal offence; that the company is not obeying the law; or covering up wrongdoing.*

(p16)

Whistleblowers are protected from victimisation in employment by the Public Interest Disclosure Act 1998. Details of disclosures which are protected are set out in the Employment Rights Act 1996. The disclosure must not be an offence under another Act (for instance, the Official Secrets Act 1989) and the person making the disclosure must reasonably believe one of the following:

- a criminal offence has been committed, is being committed or is likely to be committed;

- a person has failed, is failing or is likely to fail to comply with any legal obligation to which he or she is subject;

- a miscarriage of justice has occurred, is occurring, or is likely to occur;

- the health or safety of any individual has been, is or is likely to be endangered;

- the environment has been, is or is likely to be damaged;

- information tending to show any matter falling within any one of the preceding paragraphs has been, is or is likely to be deliberately concealed.

The College of Social Work (2013c) acknowledges potential risks of threats and lack of support for whistleblowers and has stated that it would *like to see employers not only reiterate their commitment to social workers under the PIDA 1998, but go beyond the basic requirements and take active steps to foster an open and honest culture in the workplace.*

The Francis Report in 2013, following the Mid Staffordshire NHS Foundation Trust Public Inquiry, called for better safeguards for whistleblowers and recommended the introduction of a new criminal offence of wilfully obstructing someone who is trying to raise a concern.

Public Concern at Work is an independent charity that offers support to whistle-blowers, providing free, confidential advice to anyone about crime, danger or wrongdoing at work. It also aims to promote good governance, to inform public policy, and to promote individual responsibility, organisational accountability and the public interest.

A whistleblowing helpline (08000 724 725) is available to employees and organisations in the NHS and social care sector. It is not a disclosure line, but can give advice and guidance on raising and responding to concerns and on policy development.

All organisations should have a whistleblowing policy and management interests should never override the need to share information to safeguard adults at risk of harm.

Becoming a social worker

The salience of the material in this chapter to social work with adults is again highlighted by the *Knowledge and Skills Statement* (KSS) *for Social Workers in Adult Services*. In relation to joint working it suggests that the following is expected of all social workers practising in this arena:

> Social workers should work effectively and confidently with fellow professionals in inter-agency, multi-disciplinary and interprofessional groups and demonstrate effective partnership working particularly in the context of health and social care integration and at the interface between health, children and adult social care and the third sector.

> (Department of Health, 2015, p5)

Chapter Summary

With deepening integration of health and social care and the roll-out of personal health budgets, issues of capacity and joint working will become even more important. However, despite the emphasis on partnership with people using services and their families, and with professionals from other disciplines, there will be a continuing need for workers who are prepared to be a lone voice, speaking out to advocate for the rights of individuals, and when necessary, to blow the whistle.

Further Reading

The recommendations of three serious case reviews have had particular significance for the development of policy in this area.

The Murder of Steven Hoskin (2007), Cornwall Adult Protection Committee.

Transforming Care: A national response to Winterbourne Hospital (2012), Department of Health.

Report of the Mid Staffordshire NHS Foundation Trust Public Inquiry (2013), known as the Francis Report.

A range of statistical data and case-specific information for England is published by the Health and Social Care Information Centre in its annual report. This link is to the Centre's Safeguarding Adults Return for 2013–14:

www.hscic.gov.uk/catalogue/PUB15671/sar-1314-rep.pdf

Making Safeguarding Personal (2014) provides thought-provoking guidance from the Local Government Association and the Association of Directors of Adult Social Services on developing systems for working in partnership with adults at risk and their families:

www.local.gov.uk/documents/10180/5852661/Making+Safeguarding+Personal+-+Guide+2014/4213d016-2732-40d4-bbc0-d0d8639efodf

The Home Office guidance on *Domestic Violence and Abuse* (2013, updated 2015) provides detailed and practical advice on working in this area:

www.gov.uk/domestic-violence-and-abuse

The CAADA-DASH risk assessment checklist can be found on the SafeLives website, along with other useful information:

www.safelives.org.uk

The Decision Support Tool for NHS Continuing Healthcare (Department of Health, 2012) and supporting guidance can be found at:

www.gov.uk/government/uploads/system/uploads/attachment_data/file/213139/Decision-Support-Tool-for-NHS-Continuing-Healthcare.pdf

Chapter 9

The Assessed and Supported Year in Employment

Meeting professional standards

Professional Capabilities Framework – Assessed and Supported Year in Employment (ASYE) Level Capabilities: By the end of the ASYE social workers should have consistently demonstrated practice in a wider range of tasks and roles, and have become more effective in their interventions, thus building their own confidence, and earning the confidence of others. They will have more experience and skills in relation to a particular setting and user group, and have demonstrated ability to work effectively on more complex situations. They will seek support in supervision appropriately, while starting to exercise initiative and evaluate their own practice.

Introduction

One of the developments which followed from the recommendations of the Social Work Taskforce and the Social Work Reform Board was the Assessed and Supported Year in Employment (ASYE). The first chapter of the Taskforce report suggested that the ASYE would allow social workers to *increase their expertise in specialised areas of work, building on the improved grounding provided by the degree and creating a solid platform for further career long development* (Social Work Taskforce, 2009, p7). The Social Work Reform Board then took forward that recommendation and produced detailed guidance for employers and social workers as to what an ASYE might look like. Previous separate initiatives for children and adult services – the newly qualified social worker programmes – had been evaluated positively. Graduates who experienced those programmes reported substantial increases in self-efficacy and confidence (Carpenter et al., 2011; Skills for Care, 2011) and 80 per cent of them reported being satisfied or very satisfied with their work. While new graduates have no benchmarks with which to compare their experience, the experiences of supervisors did suggest that the programmes made a difference. They reported candidates on the NQSW programmes as being better equipped for practice and that this had made a real difference to service delivery. Furthermore, a more objective measure of a significant improvement in staff retention spoke to the value of the initiatives (Carpenter et al., 2011).

Being generic, degree programmes necessarily provide breadth rather than depth in their coverage of a range of relevant subjects. A social work job role is always a specialist role to a greater or lesser degree and, once employed, a further programme of specialist training and development often follows. The ASYE framework has been helpful to social workers in the way that it has encouraged the commitments and infrastructure on the part of employers to help meet the development needs of those who are new to practice.

There are a number of texts which comprehensively cover the requirements for the ASYE and give detailed guidance and suggestions on the subject. See the Further Reading section at the end of this chapter. In this final chapter our purpose is to complement those texts by providing material which summarises certain elements covered in the book so far, and then filtering those elements through the lens of the ASYE to highlight some key themes and aspects for the newly qualified social worker.

Since the introduction of the ASYE in 2012, there have been some further important developments in social work training and education. The most significant of these in relation to adult social care is perhaps the introduction, in 2015, of the *Knowledge and Skills Statement* (KSS) *for Social Workers in Adult Services*. Reinforcing the key themes of this book, the KSS has a number of references to the particular importance of the Care Act 2014 and the Mental Capacity Act 2005. In this chapter we will also highlight how the KSS links to the ASYE and provide advice for developing the necessary knowledge and skills.

Reality shock

It is typical to reach the end of a programme of academic training and not feel quite fully prepared for making the leap into the realities of practice. Moreover, even where students feel relatively well prepared, research from a number of the caring professions suggests that 'reality shock' is common as individuals recognise that training has not, in fact, prepared them for the true realities of the experience of being in practice. It is common for the transition from student to professional to be beset by uncertainty and lack of confidence, and by perceptions of a lack of knowledge and a lack of adequate role preparation (Galpin et al., 2012).

The ASYE was developed to provide support and an extra staging post on that journey towards fully fledged independent practice. The idea was to provide greater and more consistent levels of support for those new in post, including more frequent supervision, access to specialised training and restricted caseloads.

Some continue to argue that universities are sending out graduates who are ill prepared for the realities of practice. Others recognise that, even with the best academic preparation and the best placements, it is inevitable that the newly qualified will have gaps in relevant knowledge, skills and experience. Part of the rationale for developing the ASYE framework was to help identify those gaps so that they could be more effectively filled.

Developing the habits and structures for success

In Chapter 2 we examined issues of stress and resilience. It is particularly important to consider these issues when starting a new job. The ASYE guidance is clear about what should be in place to support the newly qualified. Many employers are committed to the ASYE framework and have invested significantly to support it. A recent review found that two-thirds of supervisors/assessors had received training for their role with regard to the ASYE (Berry et al., 2013). However, workplace cultures vary significantly, and the number of experienced colleagues available to provide the necessary guidance, support and supervision also varies. Reality shock can also be coupled with role confusion or role ambiguity when new in post. A number of studies in the US and the UK have highlighted the clear links between role conflict and/ or role ambiguity and stress and burnout (Acker, 1999; Chang and Hancock, 2003). One systematic review of stress among mental health social workers in the UK found higher levels of depression and anxiety compared with normative populations and with other professions, and that role conflict and role ambiguity were widespread and clearly linked to experiences of stress (Coyle et al., 2005).

It is not uncommon for newly qualified workers to be thrown in at the deep end with high caseloads and little support. It is easy, having secured that all-important professional job, to want to make a good impression and in so doing to get sucked into unhealthy working practices. In such scenarios, having established habits for managing workloads and managing stress, the awareness and confidence to challenge bad practice become even more important.

Case Study 9.1

Julie was delighted and excited when she secured her first post in social work with an adults team. She spent the first few weeks working hard, carefully reading notes before visiting the individuals allocated to her caseload, attending meetings, writing up assessments, and preparing care and support plans. During this period she had a real sense of enthusiasm. In regular supervision sessions she discussed cases, and plans for further training and support were agreed. After two months her supervisor went off sick and the person allocated as a replacement supervisor appeared to resent the imposition of the additional workload and not to be fully present in the supervision sessions when they took place (several were cancelled at short notice). Julie noticed this person looking at the clock regularly during their sessions together. It was around this time that Julie had a couple of cases which she found difficult, due to the complexity, uncertainty and emotional impact. In both of them, differences of opinion between family members, and between other professionals about care arrangements and issues of mental capacity were evident, and there were high levels of expressed emotion and rudeness from various family members.

At this time Julie stopped going to the gym, telling herself that it was just too difficult to get there with the increased traffic levels in the area and the need to spend just that little bit of extra time on her job in order to do it really well. She also felt too tired to be bothered to do any physical exercise, and told herself that the gym sessions might not be good for the bad back that she had noticed recently. She had taken to going into the office earlier and leaving later, and to skipping lunch. When not there, she was often doing research in relation to her cases or e-mailing colleagues. She began to notice that several colleagues in the office were also sending and responding to e-mails late at night or in the early hours of the morning. Although she felt uncomfortable about it she began to join in some of the e-mail conversations which were rather negative about managers, and she began to question whether she had made the right choice in choosing this job.

Comment

In the above case study there are a number of signs of stress and burnout developing. Negativity towards colleagues and the job, fatigue, back pain and withdrawal from leisure activities may be tell-tale signs. There are responsibilities here for both the individual and those managing and supervising them. We all need to monitor ourselves and ensure that we do not sustain unhealthy working practices for too long. Employers also have a significant duty of care, which may most effectively be enacted via supervision.

Supervision

In Chapter 2 we noted the importance given to critical reflection in much of the social work literature and examined some of the links between effective practice, resilience, emotional intelligence, mindfulness and critical reflection. Ruch (2008) has emphasised the need for creating and maintaining 'reflective spaces' and supervision has the potential to be and should be one of the most important of those reflective spaces.

There have always been tensions within workplaces over the nature and role of professional supervision. Critics have pointed to the tendencies of employers to view supervision as a site of surveillance and performance management rather than one of support and personal development. A British Association of Social Workers (BASW) survey found that 70 per cent of those canvassed reported receiving insufficient emotional support in supervision sessions (BASW, 2011). While it can be difficult for a supervisor to find the right balance, good supervision can allow space for reflection and emotional support while also fulfilling managerial and administrative functions such as reviewing cases and ensuring that policies and procedures are followed (Morrison et al., 2005).

A wealth of literature testifies to the importance of good supervision in supporting and enhancing good professional practice. Provision of regular supervision is an explicit requirement of the ASYE framework. If it does not happen as it should, you should raise the issue with the appropriate manager of your service/agency.

The knowledge required for adult social care practice

The KSS for adult social work stipulates that, by the end of the Assessed and Supported Year in Employment, social workers working in an adult setting must be able to:

> *'understand and work within the legal frameworks relevant to adult settings, in particular, the Mental Capacity Act, Mental Health Act and the Care Act, and fully operate within the organisational context, policies and procedures. They will be able to confidently undertake mental capacity assessments in routine situations; to identify and work proactively and in partnership around safeguarding issues and have demonstrated the ability to work effectively in more complex situations.'*

(Department of Health, 2015, section 11)

We have covered the Mental Capacity Act and the Care Act in some detail in this text, as well as the interface with the Mental Health Act. As the House of Lords report and other investigations have found, knowledge of the Mental Capacity Act and how to implement it remains patchy. A clear understanding of how to balance the sometimes competing requirements of 'safeguarding' legislation and policy drivers with 'empowering' legislation and policy drivers also remains an ongoing challenge. Given that the Care Act is the most significant change to adult social care law in a generation, there will be little existing practice wisdom available to guide the newly qualified practitioner in the specifics of that piece of law. For these reasons, during the ASYE you may well find that your subject knowledge is ahead of that of your colleagues and supervisors and that supervision is about exploring together the new legislative landscape and exploring together how to apply the relevant law and policy to the complexities of practice.

Assessment of the ASYE

Arrangements have been in place for some time in relation to the assessment of practice of the newly qualified social worker. In 2015 the KSS for adult social work made clear the intentions of the Department of Health to introduce a *national system of quality assurance so that the profession can have confidence that employers' judgements are consistent across the country* (section 12). In order to achieve this, standardised assessment and moderation, led by Skills for Care, were proposed. It further proposed that, to ensure national consistency in the assessment of social workers at the end of their first year of practice, the ASYE assessor must be a registered social worker. Note the following required elements of assessment which are required by the end of this first year of practice:

1. three formal direct observations of practice undertaken by a registered social worker (at least two of these to be completed by the assessor);

2. at least three pieces of feedback over the course of the year from people who need care and support, or from their carers;

3. at least three pieces of feedback over the course of the year from other professionals;

4. the assessment of a written piece of work demonstrating the ability of the employee to reflect on and learn from practice: it should show how the employee has used critical reflection on their practice to improve their professional skills and demonstrate reasoned judgement relating to a practice decision;

5. the assessment of at least three examples of written reports and records, including a report written for an external decision-making processes and a set of case recordings; and

6. the assessor report.

As a qualified practitioner it may well be that your peers, service users and carers will have different expectations of you. However, the above processes are similar to those you will have experienced during qualifying training, with requirements to produce written reports, to have your practice observed by an assessor, and to demonstrate the skills of reflection and critical analysis.

Further training

The early weeks and months in a new job reveal the particular needs for further specialist training. One of the key elements of the ASYE framework is a professional development plan which should be reviewed regularly (Skills for Care, 2011). Identification of training needs will be a key element of any such plan. In such a rapidly changing legislative landscape, with elements of the landmark Care Act still to be implemented at the time of writing, employers will be providing training on such matters in order to ensure that staff in adult social care are compliant with legislation. Advice for the newly qualified includes taking advantage of as many training opportunities as possible. To ensure that your employer invests in your training it helps to present clear and reasoned applications for specific training courses and to ensure that such requests make clear the benefits of any training to the employing agency as well as to yourself.

In terms of career planning you may also wish to look beyond the horizon and consider the formal training that might provide the next rungs on the career ladder.

Two of the most common pathways for further specialist post-qualifying training are listed below. Both require two years of post-qualifying experience and the demand for people with each of these qualifications is likely to remain high for the foreseeable future.

Practice educator awards

Post-qualifying social work education is evolving and changing at the same pace as other elements of education and practice, and is responding to the same drivers for reform and development. As you will be aware from your own training, practice educators play a crucial role in shaping the next generation of practitioners. The College of Social Work has a set of standards (known as PEPS) for social work practice educators. There are two stages in the process and from October 2015 all practice educators of social work students must be registered social workers (College of Social Work, 2013a).

Best interests assessor

After two years of experience as a qualified practitioner you are eligible to undertake training as a best interests assessor (BIA). The BIA role was discussed in more detail in Chapters 5 and 6. Following a Supreme Court judgment in 2014 the demand for assessments under the DOLS regulations increased tenfold and many if not all eligible social workers in adult services are being encouraged to undertake the BIA training. The demand for this role is likely to remain very high for several years, and at least until any new recommendations from the Law Commission lead to new legislation some time after 2017.

Chapter Summary

This short chapter has revisited some of the key themes of the book, in the light of the requirements of the ASYE framework: developing the appropriate knowledge and skills base in relation to safeguarding, mental capacity and related issues pertinent to adult social care; maintaining well-being in the face of high workloads and challenging 'emotional labour'; using supervision effectively to help achieve these things; and considering career progression and further training.

We trust that, as a whole, the text has provided useful and relevant information and guidance which will assist practice in the complex world of contemporary social practice with adults.

Further Reading

Galpin, D, Bigmore, J and Parker, J (2012) *The Survival Guide for Newly Qualified Social Workers in Adult and Mental Health Services: Hitting the ground running.* London: Jessica Kingsley.

This text provides lots of useful strategies on staying motivated, managing stress and developing support networks.

Keen, S, Brown, K, Parker, J, Gray, I and Galpin, D (2012) *Newly Qualified Social Workers: A practice guide to the Assessed and Supported Year in Employment* (2nd edn) (Post-Qualifying Social Work Practice Series). Exeter: Learning Matters.

Published in 2012 after the recommendations of the reform board, including the ASYE, had been introduced, this text has remained one of the most relevant and practically useful guides for those entering social work employment for the first time. With useful practical advice on applying for jobs, using supervision effectively and managing the transition from student to practitioner, the text answers many of the questions and allays many of the fears of fledgling practitioners.

Appendix 1

Professional Capabilities Framework

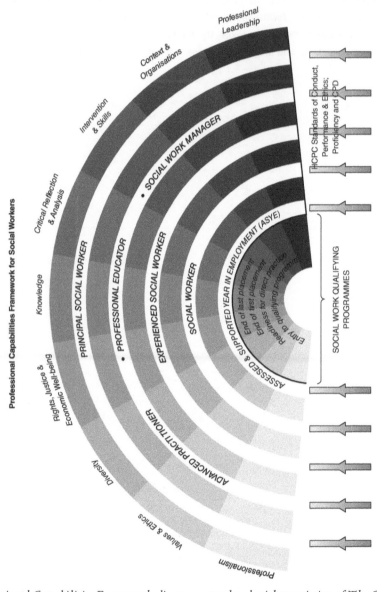

Professional Capabilities Framework diagram reproduced with permission of The College of Social Work.

References

Publications

Acker, G (1999) The impact of clients' mental illness on social workers' job satisfaction and burnout. *Health and Social Work*, 24: 112–19.

Allen, JA (1993) The constructivist paradigm: values and ethics. *Journal of Teaching in Social Work*, 8(1/2): 31–54.

Banks, S (2006) *Ethics and Values in Social Work* (3rd edn). Basingstoke: Palgrave Macmillan.

Banks, S (2012) *Ethics and Values in Social Work* (4th edn). Basingstoke: Palgrave Macmillan.

Beauchamp, TL and Childress, JF (2008) *Principles of Biomedical Ethics* (6th edn). Oxford: Oxford University Press.

Beckett, C (2006) *Essential Theory For Social Work Practice*. London: SAGE.

Beckett, C and Maynard, A (2005) *Values and Ethics in Social Work*. London: SAGE.

Berry Lound, D. and Rowe, V. (2013) *Evaluation of the Implementation of the Assessed and Supported Year in Employment (the ASYE) for Skills for Care Revised Final Report* Horsham, HOST policy research.

Birnbaum, L (2008) The use of mindfulness training to create an 'accompanying place' for social work students. *Social Work Education*, 27(8): 837–52.

Braye, S, Orr, D and Preston-Shoot, M (2015) Learning lessons about self-neglect? An analysis of serious case reviews. *Journal of Adult Protection*, 17(1): 3–18.

British Association of Social Workers (BASW) (2011) *UK Supervision Policy*. Birmingham: BASW.

British Association of Social Workers (BASW) (2012) *The Code of Ethics for Social Work*. Birmingham: BASW.

British Library (2014) *1215 Magna Carta*. London: British Library.

Britner, PA and Mossler, D (2002) Professionals' decision-making about out-of-home placements following instances of child abuse. *Child Abuse and Neglect*, 26(4): 317–32.

Brown, H and Marchant, L (2013) Using the Mental Capacity Act in complex cases. *Tizard Learning Disability Review*, 18(2): 60–9.

Brown, R and Barber, P (2008) *The Social Worker's Guide to the Mental Capacity Act*. Exeter: Learning Matters.

Brown, RE, Barber, P and Martin, D (2009) *The Mental Capacity Act 2005: A guide for practice*. Exeter: Learning Matters.

Care Act 2014. London: The Stationery Office.

Care Quality Commission (CQC) (2014) *Monitoring the Use of the Mental Capacity Act Deprivation of Liberty Safeguards in 2013/14*. Newcastle Upon Tyne: Care Quality Commission.

Carpenter, J, Patsios, D, Wood, M, Shardlow, S, Blewett, J, Platt, D, Scholar, H, Haines, C, Tunstill, J and Wong, C (2011) *Newly Qualified Social Worker Programme Evaluation Report on the Second Year (2009–10).* Available at: www.bristol.ac.uk/sps/research/projects/current/rk7035/nqswyear2.pdf.

Chang, EM and Hancock, K (2003) Role stress and role ambiguity in new nursing graduates in Australia. *Nursing & Health Sciences,* 5: 155–63.

Christopher, JC, Chrisman, JA, Trotter-Matthison, MJ, Schure, MB, Dahlen, P and Christopher, SB (2006) Perceptions of the long-term influence of mindfulness training on counselors and psychotherapists: a qualitative inquiry. *Journal of Humanistic Psychology,* 51(3): 318–49.

Clarke, J (1998) Doing the right thing? Managerialism and social welfare. In: Abbott, P and Meerabeau, L (eds) *The Sociology of the Caring Professions* (2nd edition). London: UCL Press.

The College of Social Work (2013a) *Practice Educator Professional Standards for Social Work.* London: The College of Social Work.

The College of Social Work (2013b) *Code of Ethics for Membership of the College of Social Work.* London: The College of Social Work.

The College of Social Work (2013c) An open and honest culture is needed to make whistle-blowing work (press release 2 June). Available at: www.tcsw.org.uk/pressrelease.aspx?id=6442477578.

Coyle, D, Edwards, D, Hannigan, B, Fothergill, A and Burnard, P (2005) A systematic review of stress among mental health social workers. *International Social Work,* 48(2): 201–11.

Curtis, L, Moriarty, J and Netten, A (2009) The expected working life of a social worker. *British Journal of Social Work,* advanced access, published 1 April 2010, 10.1093/bjsw/bcp039.

Data Protection Act 1998. London: The Stationery Office.

Davis, M (1980) A Multidimensional Approach to Individual Differences in Empathy. *JSAS Catalog of Selected Documents in Psychology,* 10, 85.

Department of Health (2000) *No Secrets.* London: The Stationery Office.

Department of Health (2007) *Mental Capacity Act: Code of Practice.* London: The Stationery Office.

Department of Health (2008a) *Deprivation of Liberty Safeguards: Code of Practice.* London: The Stationery Office.

Department of Health (2008b, revised 2015) *Mental Health Act 1983: Code of Practice.* London: The Stationery Office.

Department of Health (2012a) *The Decision Support Tool for NHS Continuing Healthcare.* London: The Stationery Office.

Department of Health (2012b) *Transforming Care: A national response to Winterbourne Hospital.* London: The Stationery Office.

Department of Health (2014) *Annual Report by the Chief Social Worker for Adults.* London: The Stationery Office.

Department of Health (2015) *Knowledge and Skills Statement for Social Workers in Adult Services.* London: Department of Health. Available at: www.gov.uk/government/uploads/system/uploads/attachment_data/file/411957/KSS.pdf.

Dreyfus, H and Dreyfus, S (1986) *Mind over Machine: The power of human intuition and expertise in the age of the computer.* Oxford: Basil Blackwell.

Dunn, I, Clare, H, Holland, A and Gunn, M (2007) Constructing and reconstructing 'best interests': an interpretative examination of substitute decision-making under the Mental Capacity Act 2005. *Journal of Social Welfare & Family Law,* 29(2): 117–33.

Dwyer, SM (2007) The emotional impact of social work practice. *Journal of Social Work Practice: Psychotherapeutic Approaches in Health, Welfare and the Community,* 21(1): 49–60.

Equality and Human Rights Commission (ECHR) (2010) *The United Nations Convention on the Rights of People with Disabilities: What does it mean for you?* London: ECHR .

Essex Street, *39 Essex Street Mental Capacity Law Newsletter,* April 2014.

Essex Street, *39 Essex Street Mental Capacity Law Newsletter,* May 2014.

Evans, S, Huxley, P, Webber, M, Katona, C, Gately, C, Mears, A, Medina, J, Pajak, S and Kendall, T (2005) The impact of 'statutory duties' on mental health social workers in the UK. *Health and Social Care in the Community,* 13(2): 145–54.

Flynn, M (2007) *The Murder of Steven Hoskin: A serious case review – executive summary.* Truro: Cornwall Adult Protection Committee.

Fook, J, Ryan, M and Hawkins, L (2000) *Professional Expertise: Practice, theory and education for working in uncertainty.* London: Whiting & Birch.

Forster, D (2009) Rethinking compassion fatigue as moral stress. *Journal of Ethics in Mental Health,* 4(1): 1–4.

Galpin, D, Bigmore, J and Parker, J (2012) *The Survival Guide for Newly Qualified Social Workers in Adult and Mental Health Services. Hitting the ground running.* London: Jessica Kingsley.

Gawande, A (2010) *The Checklist Manifesto: How to get things right.* New York: Metropolitan Books.

Gelsema, T, van der Doef, M, Maes, S, Janssen, M, Akerboom, S and Verhoeven, C (2006) A longitudinal study of job stress in the nursing profession: causes and consequences. *Journal of Nursing Management,* 14(4): 289–99.

Gilligan, C (1982) *In a Different Voice.* Cambridge, MA: Harvard University Press.

Gillingham, P (2011) Decision making tools and the development of expertise in child protection practitioners. Are we 'just breeding workers who are good at ticking boxes'? *Child and Family Social Work,* 16(4): 412–21.

Gorman, H (2000) Winning hearts and minds? Emotional labour and learning for care management work. *Journal of Social Work Practice,* 14(2): 149–59.

Grant, L and Kinman, G (2013) *The Importance of Emotional Resilience for Staff and Students in the 'Helping Professions': Developing an emotional curriculum.* York: The Higher Education Academy.

Grant, L and Kinman, G (2014) *Developing Resilience for Social Work Practice.* London: Palgrave Macmillan.

Gregor, C (2010) Unconscious aspects of statutory mental health social work: emotional labour and the approved mental health professional. *Journal of Social Work Practice: Psychotherapeutic Approaches in Health, Welfare and the Community,* 24(4): 429–43.

Gregory, R, Roked, F, Jines, L and Patel, A (2007) Is the degree of cognitive impairment in patients with Alzheimer's disease related to their capacity to appoint an enduring power of attorney? *Age and Ageing*, 36(5): 527–31.

Harmon, L (1990) Falling off the vine: legal fictions and the doctrine of substituted judgment. *Yale Law Journal*, 100(1): 1–71.

Health and Social Care Information Centre (HSCIC) (2014) *Safeguarding Adults Return*. Exeter: HSCIC.

Health & Care Professions Council (2012) *Standards of Conduct, Performance and Ethics*. London: HCPC.

HM Government (2014) *Valuing Every Voice, Respecting Every Right: Making the case for the Mental Capacity Act. The Government's response to the House of Lords Select Committee Report on the Mental Capacity Act 2005*. London: The Stationery Office.

Holder, A and Jolley, D (2012) Forced relocation between nursing homes: residents' health outcomes and potential moderators. *Reviews in Clinical Gerontology*, 22(4): 301–19.

Home Office (2013, updated 2015) *Domestic Violence and Abuse. Available at: www.gov.uk/domestic-violence-and-abuse*.

Hotopf, M. (2013) The Assessment of Mental Capacity.In Jacob,R., Gunn,M. And Holland, A. *Mental Capacity Legislation. Principles and Practice*. London, Royal College of Psychiatrists.

House of Lords Select Committee on the Mental Capacity Act 2005 (2013a) *Oral and Written Evidence – Volume 1 (A–K)*. London. The Stationery Office. Available at: www.parliament.uk/documents/lords-committees/mental-capacity-act/mental-capacity-act-2005-vol1.pdf

House of Lords Select Committee on the Mental Capacity Act 2005 (2013b) *Oral and Written Evidence – Volume 2 (L–W)*. London. The Stationery Office. Available at: www.parliament.uk/documents/Mental-Capacity-Act-2005/mental-capacity-act-2005-vol2.pdf

House of Lords Select Committee on the Mental Capacity Act 2005 (2014) *Mental Capacity Act 2005: Post-legislative scrutiny*. London: The Stationery Office.

Hugman, R (2005) *New Approaches in Ethics for the Caring Professions*. London: Palgrave Macmillan.

Human Rights Act 1998 (c42). London: The Stationery Office.

Jackson, P (2011) in *London Borough of Hillingdon v Steven Neary and Ors* [2011] EWHC 1377 (COP).

Jackson, P (2013) in *Re M (Best Interests: Deprivation of Liberty)* [2013] EWHC 3456 (COP).

Joint Committee of the House of Lords and House of Commons (2003) *Draft Mental Incapacity Bill*. London: The Stationery Office.

Jones, R (2008) *Mental Capacity Act Manual* (3rd edn). Andover: Sweet & Maxwell.

Jones, R (2012) *Mental Capacity Act Manual* (5th edn). Andover: Sweet & Maxwell.

Kabat-Zinn, J (1994) *Wherever You Go, There You Are: Mindfulness meditation in everyday life*. New York: Hyperion Books.

Kahneman, D (2012) *Thinking Fast and Slow*. London: Penguin.

Kinman, G and Grant, L (2010) Exploring stress resilience in trainee social workers: the role of emotional and social competencies. *British Journal of Social Work*, 41: 261–75.

Kirkman, E and Melrose, K (2014) *Clinical Judgement and Decision-Making in Children's Social Work: An analysis of the 'front door' system.* London: UK Government Department for Education.

Laming, H (2009) *The Protection of Children in England: A progress report.* London: House of Commons.

Law Commission (1991) *Mentally Incapacitated Adults and Decision-making: An overview. Consultation Paper No. 119.* London: HMSO.

Law Society (1989) *Decision Making and Mental Incapacity: A discussion document.* London: The Law Society's Mental Health Sub-Committee.

Leeson, C (2010) The emotional labour of caring about looked-after children. *Child and Family Social Work*, 15(4): 483–91.

Lloyd, C, King, R and Chenoweth, L (2002) Social work, stress and burnout: a review. *Journal of Mental Health*, 11(3): 255–65.

Local Government Association and the Association of Directors of Adult Social Services (2014) *Making Safeguarding Personal.* London: LGA and ADASS.

Lueke, A and Gibson, B (2014) Mindfulness meditation reduces implicit age and race bias: the role of reduced automaticity of responding. *Social Psychological & Personality Science*, 6: 284–91.

Lyons, D (2010) Different laws, same principles: mental health and incapacity legislation across the UK. *Advances in Psychiatric Treatment*, 16: 158–60.

Mantell, A and Scragg, T (2009) *Safeguarding Adults in Social Work.* Exeter: Learning Matters.

Maslach, C (2003) *Burnout: The Cost of Caring.* Los Altos, CA: Malor Books.

Mather, M and Lighthall, N (2012) Both risk and reward are processed differently in decisions made under stress. *Current Directions in Psychological Science*, 21(2): 36–41.

McGarrigle, T and Walsh, C (2011) Mindfulness, self-care, and wellness in social work: effects of contemplative training. *Journal of Religion and Spirituality in Social Work*, 30(3): 212–33.

McNicoll, A (2014) Six ways councils are trying to combat a shortage of best interests assessors. *Community Care*, 1 October.

Mental Capacity Act 2005 (c9). London: The Stationery Office.

Mental Health Act 1983 (c20). London: The Stationery Office.

Mental Health Act 2007 (c12). London: The Stationery Office.

Mid Staffordshire NHS Foundation Trust (2013) *Report of the Mid Staffordshire NHS Foundation Trust Public Inquiry.* London: The Stationery Office.

Mill, JS (1909) *On Liberty.* New York: Collier & Son.

Miller, JG (1984) Culture and the development of everyday social explanation. *Journal of Personality and Social Psychology*, 46(5): 961–78.

Mishna, F and Bogo, M (2007) Reflective practice in contemporary social work classrooms. *Journal of Social Work Education*, 43(3): 529–41.

Morrison, T, Hathaway, J and Fairley, G (2005) *Staff Supervision in Social Care: Making a real difference for staff and service users.* Brighton: Pavilion Publishing.

Munro, E (1999) Common errors of reasoning in child protection work. *Child Abuse and Neglect,* 23(8): 745–58.

Munro, E (2008) Lessons from research on decision-making. In: Lindsey, D and Shlonsky, A (eds) *Child Welfare Research: Advances for practice and policy.* Oxford: Oxford University Press.

Munro, E (2011) *The Munro Review of Child Protection: Final report – a child-centred system.* Available at: www.education.gov.uk/munroreview/downloads/8875_DFE_MunroReport_Tagged.pdf.

National Health Service and Community Care Act 1990 (c19). London: The Stationery Office.

Official Secrets Act 1989. London: The Stationery Office.

Okai, D, Owen, G, McGuire, H, Singh, S, Churchill, R and Hotopf, M (2007) Mental capacity in psychiatric patients: a systematic review. *British Journal of Psychiatry,* 191: 291–97.

O'Sullivan, T (2010) *Decision Making and Social Work* (2nd edition). Basingstoke: Palgrave Macmillan.

Parton, N (2001) Risk and professional judgement. In: Cull, L-A and Roche, J (eds), *The Law and Social Work.* Basingstoke: Palgrave Macmillan.

Pearcey, P and Elliott, B (2004) Student impressions of clinical nursing. *Nurse Education Today,* 24(5): 382–7.

Pitblado, A (2013) *The decision of the Court of Appeal in (1) PC and (2) NC v City of York* [2013] EWCA.

Police and Criminal Evidence Act 1984. London: The Stationery Office.

Preston-Shoot, M and Wrigley, V (2002) Closing the circle: social workers' responses to multi agency procedures on older age abuse. *British Journal of Social Work,* 32: 299–320.

Public Interest Disclosure Act 1998. London: The Stationery Office.

Ruch, G (2008) *Post Qualifying Child Care Social Work: Developing reflective practice.* London: SAGE.

Rushton, A. (1987). Stress amongst social workers. In Payne,R. and Firth-Cozens,J. (Eds.), *Stress in Health Professionals,* 167–188. Chichester, John Wiley & Sons.

Safeguarding Vulnerable Groups Act 2006. London: The Stationery Office.

Series, L (2012) *DOLS v Guardianship – Summary and discussion* [blog entry] 4 January. Available at: http://thesmallplaces.blogspot.co.uk/2012/01/3-dols-v-guardianship-discussion.html.

Sexual Offences Act 2003. London: The Stationery Office.

Shalock, R, Baker, P and Croser, M (2002) *Embarking on a New Century: Mental retardation at the end of the 20th century.* Washington, DC: American Association on Mental Retardation.

Shapiro, S, Brown, KW and Biegel, GM (2007) Teaching self-care to caregivers: effects of mindfulness-based stress reduction on the mental health of therapists in training. *Training and Education in Professional Psychology,* 1(2): 105–15.

Shapiro, S, Jazaleri, H and Goldin, P (2012) Mindfulness-based stress reduction effects on moral reasoning and decision making. *Journal of Positive Psychology,* 7(6): 504–15.

Shier, ML and Graham, JR (2011) Mindfulness, subjective well-being, and social work: insight into their interconnection from social work practitioners. *Social Work Education*, 30(1): 29–44.

Siebert, DC (2005) Personal and occupational factors in burnout among practicing social workers. *Journal of Social Service Research*, 32(2): 25–44.

Skills for Care (2011) *Getting a Good Start: Evaluation of the first year of the Newly Qualified Social Worker framework for adult services, 2009/10*. Leeds: Skills for Care. Available at: www.skillsforcare.org.uk/nmsruntime/saveasdialog.aspx?lID=11162&sID=2682.

Skills for Care (2013a) *Code of Conduct for Healthcare Support Workers and Adult Social Care Workers in England*. Leeds: Skills for Care.

Skills for Care (2013b) *National Minimum Training Standards for Healthcare Support Workers and Adult Social Care Workers in England*. Leeds: Skills for Care.

Social Work Taskforce (2009) *Building a Safe, Confident Future: Final report of the Social Work Taskforce*. London: The Stationery Office.

Starcke, K and Brand, M (2012) Decision making under stress: a selective review. *Neuroscience and Biobehavioral Review*, 36(1): 1228–48.

Sutherland, NS (1992) *Irrationality: Why we don't think straight*. New York: Rutgers University Press.

Szerletics, A (2012) *Best Interests Decision Making under the Mental Capacity Act*. Essex Autonomy Project. Available at: http://autonomy.essex.ac.uk/best-interests-decision-making-under-the-mental-capacity-act.

Taleb, N (2001) *Fooled by Randomness*. New York: Random House.

Tessman, L (2005) *Burdened Virtues: Virtue ethics for liberatory struggles*. New York: Oxford University Press.

Texeira, C, Ribeiro, O, Fonseca, A and Carvalho, A (2014) Ethical decision making in intensive care units: a burnout risk factor? Results from a multicentre study conducted with physicians and nurses. *Journal of Medical Ethics*, 40(2): 97–103.

Tham, P and Meagher, G (2009) Working in human services: how do experiences and working conditions in child welfare social work compare? *British Journal of Social Work*, 39(5): 807–27.

Torke AM, Alexander, GC and Lantos, J (2008) Substituted judgment: the limitations of autonomy in surrogate decision making. *Journal of General Internal Medicine*, 23(9): 1514–17.

Tversky, A and Kahneman, D (1982) Judgement under uncertainty: heuristics and biases. In: Kahneman, D, Stovic, P and Tversky, A (eds) *Judgement Under Uncertainty: Heuristics and biases*. Cambridge: Cambridge University Press.

United Nations (2006) *Social Justice in an Open World: The role of the United Nations*. New York: United Nations.

Wendt, S and Seymour, S (2010) Applying post-structural ideas to empowerment: implications for social work education. *Social Work Education*, 29(6): 670–82.

Wendt,S., Tuckey,M., and Prosser, B. (2011) Thriving, not just surviving in emotionally demanding fields of practice. *Health and Social Care in the Community*, 19, 3, 317–325

Williams, J and Netten, A (2003) *Guidelines for the Closure of Care Homes for Older People: Prevalence and content of local government protocols.* Canterbury: Personal Social Services Research Unit.

Wilson, G and Kelly, B (2012) *Enhancing Social Work Students' Learning Experience and Readiness to Undertake Practice Learning.* York: The Higher Education Academy Subject Centre for Social Policy and Social Work.

Case law

Aintree University Hospitals NHS Foundation Trust v James [2013] UKSC 67 (AC)

AM v South London and Maudsley NHS Foundation Trust and others [2013] UKUT 0365 (AAC)

Austin v UK [2012] 55 EHRR 14 (ECtHR)

Bolam v Friern Hospital Management Committee [1957] 1 W.L.R. 582

County Durham and Darlington NHSFT v PP & Ors [2014] EWCOP 9.

D v R (the Deputy of S) and S [2010] EWHC 2405 (COP)

Frenchay Healthcare NHS Trust v S [1994] 2 All ER 403

HL v UK [2004] ECHR 471 (EctHR)

London Borough of Hillingdon v Steven Neary and Ors [2011] EWHC 1377 (COP)

Norfolk CC v PB [2014] EWCOP 14.

Northamptonshire Healthcare NHS Foundation Trust & Anor v ML (Rev 1) [2014] EWCOP 2

P (by his litigation friend the Official Solicitor) v Cheshire West and Chester Council & Anor [2014] UKSC 19

Portsmouth NHS Trust v Wyatt & Ors [2004] EWHC 2247 (Fam)

R v Bournewood Community and Mental Health NHS Trust ex parte L [1998] 3 ALL ER 289

Re F (Mental Patient: Sterilisation) [1990] 2 A.C.1

Re SL (Adult Patient) (Medical Treatment) [2001] (Fam)

Re Y [1996] 2 FLR 791

Wyatt v Portsmouth NHS Trust (No 3) [2005] EWHC 693 (Fam)

Index